实用英语写作

李丽 陈辛欣 著

清华大学出版社
北京

内容简介

本书以《大学英语教学指南（2020版）》为依据，强调英文写作的实践性和实用性。全书分为四大部分：第一部分为写作的基本原理，内容包括字、句、段的写作技巧和展开方法；第二部分为社交信函，内容包括多种工作和日常社交中的应用文的写作方法；第三部分为商务信函，介绍了商务交往中比较常见的信函、通知等的写作格式、要求和方法；第四部分为学术写作，主要介绍了学术论文的组成部分、结构和各个部分的写作策略。以上四个部分，均包含了写作范式的说明，列举了大量范例，并提供了相应的范例分析，供学生研读和模仿。每一个单元涉及一个文体或知识点，总结并列举了该写作类型常用的字、词、短语和句等，供学习者参考使用。书中配有丰富的写作练习，以方便学习者实操训练。

本书可作为高校英语专业写作课的教材使用，也可作为英语爱好者进行自我提升的阅读材料使用。

本书封面贴有清华大学出版社防伪标签，无标签者不得销售。
版权所有，侵权必究。举报：010-62782989，beiqinquan@tup.tsinghua.edu.cn。

图书在版编目 (CIP) 数据

实用英语写作 / 李丽，陈辛欣 著 . —— 北京：清华大学出版社，2025.2
ISBN 978-7-302-56964-0

Ⅰ．①实… Ⅱ．①李…②陈… Ⅲ．①英语—写作—高等学校—教材 Ⅳ．① H319.36

中国版本图书馆 CIP 数据核字 (2020) 第 230467 号

责任编辑：陈立静
装帧设计：杨玉兰
责任校对：常　婷
责任印制：刘海龙

出版发行：清华大学出版社
　　　网　　址：https://www.tup.com.cn, https://www.wqxuetang.com
　　　地　　址：北京清华大学学研大厦 A 座　　邮　编：100084
　　　社　总　机：010-83470000　　邮　购：010-62786544
　　　投稿与读者服务：010-62776969, c-service@tup.tsinghua.edu.cn
　　　质量反馈：010-62772015, zhiliang@tup.tsinghua.edu.cn
印 装 者：三河市龙大印装有限公司
经　　销：全国新华书店
开　　本：185mm×260mm　　印　张：13.5　　字　数：236 千字
版　　次：2025 年 2 月第 1 版　　印　次：2025 年 2 月第 1 次印刷
定　　价：49.80 元

产品编号：078344-01

前　言

  2020年10月，教育部颁布了《大学英语教学指南（2020版）》（以下简称《大学英语教学指南》），针对学生英文书面表达能力，制定了培养目标。

  其中，基础目标为："能用英语描述个人经历、观感、情感和发生的事件等。能写常见的应用文，能就一般性话题或提纲，以短文的形式展开简短的讨论、解释、说明等，语言结构基本完整，中心思想明确，用词恰当，语意连贯。"

  提高目标为："能撰写所学专业论文摘要和英语小论文；""能用英语对未来所从事工作或岗位的职能、业务、产品等进行简要的书面介绍，语言表达内容完整，观点明确，条理清楚，语句通顺"。

  发展目标为："能就专业话题撰写简短报告或论文，""能以适当的格式和文体撰写商务信函、简讯、备忘录等。能恰当地运用写作技巧。"

  写作能力是人的认知能力、思考能力和文字运用能力的综合反映，因此是训练难度最大的课程。本书旨在通过大量实践训练，为英语学习者实用英语写作能力的精进提供有效帮助。

  从《大学英语教学指南》对于写作能力的分级培养目标来看，学生应具备的写作技能包括：应用文的书写，特别是商务信函、简讯等的书面表达；与专业相关的英文论文、报告或者业务、产品介绍等的书面表达。

  本书以《大学英语教学指南》为依据，强调英文写作的实践性和实用性。全书分为四大部分：第一部分为写作的基本原理（Principles of English Writing），内容包括字、句、段的写作技巧和展开方法；第二部分为社交信函（Social Letters），内容

i

前　言

包括多种工作和日常社交中的应用文的书写方法；第三部分为商务信函（Business Correspondence），介绍了商务交往中比较常见的信函、通知等的写作格式、要求和方法；第四部分为学术写作（Research Paper），主要介绍了学术论文的组成部分、结构和各个部分的写作策略。

以上四个部分，均包含了写作范式的说明，列举了大量范例，并提供了相应的范例分析，供学生研读和模仿。每一个单元涉及一个文体或知识点，总结并列举了该写作类型常用的字、词、短语和句等，供学习者参考使用。书中配有丰富的写作练习，方便学习者实操训练。在本书的编写过程中，力求做到内容新颖、选材有趣、语言地道、易于模仿。

本书课件，可扫描本页下方二维码进行下载。

本书的出版得到了清华大学出版社的大力支持，在此表示衷心感谢。由于编者水平有限，书中难免存在疏漏与不足之处，恳请广大读者不吝赐教。

编　者
2024 年 11 月

目 录

Chapter 1 Principles of English Writing ································ 1

    Unit 1 Word Choice ··· 3

    Unit 2 Sentence Effectiveness ································· 12

    Unit 3 Paragraph Development ······························ 21

Chapter 2 Social Letters ··· 31

    Unit 4 Invitations ·· 35

    Unit 5 Thank-you Letters ······································ 41

    Unit 6 Apologies ·· 46

    Unit 7 Congratulations ··· 51

    Unit 8 Application ·· 56

    Unit 9 Résumé ··· 62

    Unit 10 Recommendation ····································· 71

Chapter 3 Business Correspondence ························· 79

    Unit 11 Requests and Inquiries ······························ 82

    Unit 12 Orders ·· 89

    Unit 13 Complaints ·· 96

目 录

Unit 14　Appreciation ·· 102

Unit 15　Refusal ··· 107

Chapter 4　Research Paper ································ 113

Unit 16　Introduce the Study ·· 115

Unit 17　Develop Literature Review ··· 130

Unit 18　State the Methodology ··· 140

Unit 19　Present Results and Findings ·· 154

Unit 20　Compose Discussion/Conclusion ······································ 166

Unit 21　Write the Abstract ·· 178

Reference Answers ·· 188

Principles of English Writing

Writing is a process in which thinking and learning take place. This process is known as the writing-thinking-learning connection. It's a process that results in a communicative product that conforms to grammatical, syntactical, mechanical, and genre conventions. Significantly, writing also performs recognizable social functions that have increased in importance with the rise of social media.

Writing success is highly dependent on learning and adapting to the implicit rules and genre conventions of a discourse.

To understand the conventions, writers need excellent materials to imitate, or to emulate. They need to be able to identify errors that characterize non-standard English. They need to be able to identify rectifiable weaknesses. They need to be able to discern perspectives, inaccuracies, biases, gaps, and blind spots. They need to be able to identify and analyze the rhetorical and stylistic devices that accomplish writers' use. They also need to be able to analyze, evaluate, and select information, and structure and synthesize the information into logical, meaningful, economical and persuasive writings of their own. Much of this competence not only comes from writing instruction by knowledgeable teachers, but also comes from the process of reading and writing. This chapter will share the principles of language use in writings.

Word Choice

One key factor that determines excellent writing style is how well your choice of words matches your readers' expectations, which depends on who those readers are. In formal writing—for example, at university or in the workplace—you need to adhere quite strictly to the conventions of academic and professional writing. If you are writing creatively, you will have a much wider choice in relation to words and can be as imaginative and distinctive as you like. The three central concepts in word usage are style, voice, and tone, with their related concepts of different scope of usage.

Style is generally judged on a writer's choice and command of words and syntax (sentence structure). Voice is what creates your relationship with your readers: what "comes through" about you by your writing, and how you present yourself to your readers. Your readers "hear" your voice and construct your character. Voice is what makes a writer distinctive. Your voice may be authoritative, reassuring, avuncular, sincere, humble, opinionated, knowledgeable, and idiosyncratic. Your purpose of writing affects the voice that you were aiming for. Tone is what creates the effect of your message on your readers. It is always subjective, that is, open to different interpretations by different readers. However, most readers share the opinion that a communication can be cold or friendly, condescending or sincere.

The English language contains over a half million words. However, such a wide choice can make you wonder all the time which choice is best or how to choose.

Word choice can make an enormous difference in the quality of your writing for at least one obvious reason: if you substitute an incorrect or vague word for the right one, you will risk being misunderstood. To help you avoid possible indecision over word choice, this unit offers some practical suggestions for selecting words.

Selecting the Correct Words

Language has been classified into three categories, or levels, of usage: (1) colloquial, (2) informal, and (3) formal.

Colloquial language is the kind of speech you use most often in conversation with your friends, classmates, and family. It may not always be grammatically correct (e.g."it's me"); it may include fragments, contractions, some slangs, words identified as non-standard by the dictionary (such as "yuck" or "lousy"), and shortened or abbreviated words (e.g."grad school", "LOL"). Colloquial speech is everyday language. Although it can be used in some writings such as text messages, personal e-mails and letters, journals, and so forth, you should think carefully about using colloquial language in most college essays or in professional letters, reports, or papers because such a choice implies a causal relationship between the writer and the reader.

Informal language is called-for in most college and professional assignments. The tone is more formal than in colloquial writing or speech, and no slang or non-standard words are permissible. Informal writing consistently uses correct grammar; fragments are used for special effects or not at all. Most of your essays in English classes will be written in informal language.

Formal language is found in important documents and serious speeches. Formal writing often uses inverted word order and balanced sentence structure. Most people rarely need to write formally, however, if you are called on to do so, be careful to avoid diction that sounds pretentious, pompous, or phony.

Selecting the Best Words

In addition to selecting the correct words and appropriate tone, good writers choose words that firmly plant their ideas in the minds of their readers. The best prose not only makes cogent points but also states these points memorably. To help you select the best words to express your ideas, the following is a list of problems of word choice in students' writing today.

1. Do make your words as precise as possible.

"The big tree was hit by lightning" for example, is not as formative or interesting as "Lightning splintered the neighbors' thirty-foot oak". Don't use words whose meanings are unclear:

Vague Verbs

Unclear: She got involved in a lawsuit. [How?]
Clear: She is suing her dentist for filling the wrong tooth.

Unclear: Tom can relate to Jennifer. [What's the relationship?]
Clear: Tom understands Jennifer's financial problem.
Unclear: He won't deal with his ex-wife. [In what way?]
Clear: He refuses to speak to his ex-wife.

Vague Nouns

Unclear: The burglar took several valuable things from our house. [What items?]
Clear: The burglar took a television, a tablet, and a microwave oven from our house.
Unclear: When I have my car serviced, there is always trouble. [What kind?]
Clear: When I have my car serviced, the mechanics always find additional repairs and never have the car ready when it is promised.

Vague Modifiers

Unclear: His terrible explanation left me very confused. [Why "terrible"? How confused?]
Clear: His disorganized explanation left me too confused to begin the project.
Unclear: The boxer hit the punching bag really hard. [How hard?]
Clear: The boxer hit the punching bag so hard that it split open.
Unclear: Casablanca is a good movie with something for everyone. [Why "good" and for everyone?]
Clear: Casablanca is a witty, sentimental movie that successfully combines an adventure story and a romance.

To help you recognize the difference between general and specific language, consider the following series of words:

General → → → → → → → → → → → → → → → → Specific

food → *snack food* → *chips* → *potato chips* → *Red Hot Jalapeño Potato Chips*

car → *red car* → *red sports car* → *classic red Corvette* → *1966 red Corvette convertible*

building → *house* → *old house* → *big old fancy house* → *19th–century Victorian mansion*

The preceding examples illustrate varying degrees of generality, with the words becoming more specific as they move to the right. Sometimes in your writing you will, of course, need to use general words to communicate your thought. However, most writers need to practice finding specific language to substitute for bland, vague, or overly general diction that doesn't clearly present the precise picture the writer has in mind. For instance, look at the difference between these two sentences:

1) My date arrived at the restaurant in an old car and then surprised us by ordering snack food.

2) My date arrived at the restaurant in a rusted-out 52 Cadillac DeVille without bumper and then surprised us by ordering a large, expensive bowl of imported cheese puffs.

Which description better conveys the start of an unusual evening? Which sentence would make you want to hear more?

Not all the occasions call for specific details. Don't add details that merely clutter if they aren't important to the idea or mood you are creating.

Most of the time, writers can improve their drafts by giving their language a close look, considering places where a vigorous verb or a "showing" adjective or a specific noun might make an enormous difference to the reader. As you revise and polish your own essays, ask yourself if you can clarify and enliven your writing by replacing dull, lifeless words with engaging, vivid, specific ones. Challenge yourself to find the best words possible—it's a writing habit that produces effective, reader-pleasing results.

2. Do make your word choice as fresh and original as possible.

Instead of saying "My hometown is very quiet", you might say, "My hometown's definition of an orgy is a light burning after midnight." In other words, if you can make your readers admire and remember your prose, you have a better chance of persuading them to accept your ideas.

Conversely, don't fill your sentences with clichés that may cause your writing to sound lifeless and trite, because (1) they are often vague or imprecise, and (2) they are used so frequently that they rob your prose style of personality and uniqueness.

Novice writers often include trite expressions because they do not recognize them as clichés; therefore, here is a partial list of phrases to avoid. Instead of using a cliché, try substituting an original phrase to describe what you see or feel.

crack of dawn	needle in a haystack	gentle as a lamb
a crying shames	bed of roses	blind as a bat
white as a sheet	cold as ice	strong as an ox
depths of despair	hard as nails	sober as a judge
dead of night	white as snow	didn't sleep a wink
shadow of a doubt	almighty dollar	face the music
hear a pin drop	busy as a bee	out like a light
blessed event	to make a long story	the last straw
first and foremost	short pale as a ghost	solid as a rock

It would be impossible to memorize all the clichés and trite expressions, but do check your prose for recognizable, overworked phrases so that your words will not be predictable and, consequently dull. If you aren't sure whether a phrase is a cliché, but you've heard that it is used frequently, your prose will probably be stronger if you substitute an original phrase for the suspected one.

For example, it's easy to recognize such overused phrases as "last but not least", "easier said than done", and "when all was said and done". But they may pop up in essays almost without a writer's awareness. For instance, using your very first thoughts, fill in the blanks in the following sentence:

After years of service, my old car finally _____, _____, and_____ by the side of the road.

If your immediate responses were the three words: "coughed, sputtered, and died", don't be surprised! The writer describing the car wants readers to see the particular old car, not some bland image identically reproduced in readers' minds. As a writer, you also want your readers to "see" your specific idea and be engaged by your prose rather than skipping over canned-bland images.

3. Do select simple, direct words that your readers can easily understand.

Don't use pompous or pseudo-sophisticated language in place of plain speech. Wherever possible, avoid jargon—that is, words and phrases that are unnecessarily technical, pretentious, or abstract.

Technical jargon—terms specific to one area of study or specialization—should be omitted or clearly defined in essays directed to a general audience because such language is often inaccessible to anyone outside the writer's particular field. Although most professions do have their own terms, you should limit your use of specialized language to writing aimed solely at your professional colleagues; always try to avoid technical jargon in prose directed at a general audience. To avoid such verbal litter in your own writing, follow these rules:

1) Always select the plainest, most direct words you know.

Jargon: The editor wanted to halt the proliferation of the product because she discovered an error on the page that terminates the volume.

Revised: The editor wanted to stop publishing the book because she found an error on the last page.

2) Replace nominalizations (nouns that are made from verbs and adjectives, usually by adding endings such as -tion, -ism, -ness, or -al) with simpler verbs and nouns.

Jargon: The departmental head has come to the recognition that the utilization of verbose verbalization renders informational content inaccessible.

Revised: The head of the department recognizes that wordiness confuses meaning.

3) Avoid adding -ize or -wise to verbs and adverbs.

Jargon: Weatherwise, it looked like a good day to finalize her report on wind tunnels.

Revised: The day's clear weather would help her finish her report on wind tunnels.

4) Abandon meaningless words such as "factor", "aspect", and "situation".

Jargon: The convenience factor of the neighborhood grocery store is one aspect of its success.

Revised: The convenience of the neighborhood grocery store contributes to its success.

Remember that a good writing is clear and direct, never wordy, cloudy, or ostentatious.

4. Do enliven your writing with figurative language when appropriate.

Figurative language produces pictures or images in a reader's mind, often by comparing something unfamiliar to something familiar. The most common two figurative devices are the simile and the metaphor. A simile is a comparison between two people, places, feelings, or things, using the word "like" or "as"; a more forceful comparison, omitting the word "like" or "as", is a metaphor. Here are two examples:

Simile: George eats his meals like a hog.

Metaphor: George is a hog at mealtime.

In both sentences, George, whose eating habits are unfamiliar to the reader, is likened to a hog, whose sloppy manners are generally well known. By comparing George to a hog, the writer gives the reader a clear picture of George at the table. Figurative language can not only help you present your ideas in clear, concrete, economical ways but also make your prose more memorable—especially when the image or picture you present is a fresh, arresting one. Here are some examples of striking images designed to catch the reader's attention and to clarify the writer's point:

- An hour away from him felt like a month in the country.
- The atmosphere of the meeting room was as tense as a World Series game tied in the ninth inning.
- The woman's earrings were as big as butter plates.
- The angry accusation flew like a spear, once thrown, it could not be retrieved and it cut deeply.
- Behind her broad polished desk, Matilda was a queen bee with a swarm of office drones buzzing at her door.
- The factory squatted on the bank of the river like a huge black toad.

Figurative language can spice up your prose, but like any spice, it can be misused, thus spoiling your soup. Therefore, don't overuse figurative language since not every point needs a metaphor or simile for clarity or emphasis. Too many images are confusing. Moreover, don't use stale images. If you can't catch your readers' attention with a fresh picture, don't bore them with a stale one.

5. Do vary your word choice so that your prose does not sound wordy, repetitious, or monotonous.

Consider the following sentence:

According to child psychologists, depriving a child of sensory stimulation in the earliest stages of childhood can cause the child brain damage.

Reworded, the following sentence eliminates the tiresome, unnecessary repetition of the word "child":

According to child psychologists, depriving infants of sensory stimulation can cause brain damage.

By omitting or changing repeated words, you can add variety and crispness to your prose. Of course, don't ever change your words or sentence structure to achieve variety at the expense of clarity or precision. At all times, your goal is to make your prose clear to your readers.

6. Do remember that wordiness is a major problem for all writers, even the professionals.

State your thoughts directly and specifically in as few words as necessary to communicate your meaning clearly.

In addition to the advice given above on avoiding wordy or vague jargon, euphemisms, and clichés, you might also want to know some other tips of choosing right words:

7. Avoid sexist language.

8. Do call things by their proper names.

9. Refrain from using texting language in your academic or professional writing.

10. Don't use trendy expressions or slangs in your essays.

Exercises

I. Underline the vague nouns, verbs, and modifiers in the sentences below. Then rewrite each sentence so that it says something clear and specific.

1. The experiment had very bad results.

2. The speaker came up with some odd items.

3. The house was big, old, and ugly.

4. The man is a nice guy with a good personality.

5. I felt that the whole ordeal was quite an experience.

6. The machine we got was missing a few things.

7. The woman was really something special.

8. The classroom material wasn't interesting.

9. The child made a lot of very loud noises.

10. The cost of the unusual meal was amazing.

II. Rewrite the following sentences, eliminating all clichés, slang, mixed metaphors, and euphemisms; change any texting or sexist language you find.

1. Anyone who wants to be elected the next congressman from our state must clearly recognize that our tourist industry is sitting on a launching pad, ready to flex its muscles and become a dynamo.

2. I thought the whole deal was sweet, but then my sister goes "whatever"; I think she got a special delivery from the duh truck. G2G, thx, Dude!

3. After all is said and done, agricultural producers may be forced to relocate to urban environments, settling in substandard housing with other members of the disadvantaged class until the day they expire.

4. Both Ron Howard and Shirley Temple were popular child actors; careerwise, Howard moved on to directing movies, but Shirley left show biz to serve Old Glory by becoming ambassadoress to Ghana and Czechoslovakia.

5. Each commander realizes that one day he might be called upon to use the peacekeepers to depopulate an emerging nation in a lethal intervention.

6. Although Jack once regarded Jill as sweet and innocent, he knew then and there that she was really a wolf in sheep's clothing with a heart of stone.

7. The city councilman was stewing in his juices when he learned that his goals-impaired son had been arrested for fooling around with the funds for the fiscal underachievers' home.

8. NVR rite lik ds n yr skool r prowork. Srsly. Tlk 2 u l8r. (Never write like this in your school for professional work. Seriously. Talk to you later.)

9. At a press conference on the war in Iraq, former Defense Secretary Donald Rumsfeld announced the following: "Reports that say something hasn't happened are always interesting to me, because as we know, there are known knowns, there are things we know we know. We also know there are known unknowns; that is to say we know there are some things we do not know. But there are also unknown unknowns—the ones we don't know we don't know."

III. Fill in the blanks with colorful words. You may make the paragraph as exciting or humorous as you wish but avoid clichés. Make your responses as original and creative as possible.

As midnight approached, Janet and Brad _____ toward the _____ mansion to escape the _____ storm. Their _____ car had _____ on the road nearby. The night was _____, and Brad _____ at the shadows with _____ and _____. As they _____ up the _____ steps to the _____ door, the _____ wind was filled with _____ and _____ sounds. Janet _____ on the door, and moments later, it opened to reveal the _____ scientist, with a face like a _____. Brad and Janet _____ at each other and then _____ (complete this sentence and then end the paragraph and the story).

IV. Rewrite the following passage and delete unnecessary words.

1. The tricolor pottery of the Tang dynasty is best known among people for its exquisite designs, brilliant colors, and vivid images. Making the pottery involves more than 30 processes, which is quite a large number. Baked twice at different temperatures, the clay bases are accented with soft glazes in the colors of amber, green and yellow. Tang pottery was used mainly as burial objects for the dead in ancient China, a custom that has kept many of these old and ancient relics from being destroyed across the centuries that have passed since they were first made so long ago. Each year, archaeologists unearth from the ground more magnificent works from the period of the Tang dynasty. These priceless works are part of China's priceless artistic heritage.

2. If you wish to experience a traditional time-honored Chinese celebration, there are few better choices you can make than the Dragon Boat Festival that falls on the fifth day of the fifth lunar month. This annual event started as part of a ceremonial ritual to commemorate the death of Qu Yuan, a minister of the government during the Warring States period, who is revered and esteemed for his integrity and patriotism. Dragon boat races are the most excitingly thrilling part of the festival, drawing huge crowds of spectators who watch them. Dragon boats are simply canoes that are decorated to look like open-mouthed dragons. The longest boats are powered by as many as 80 strong rowers.

Sentence Effectiveness

To improve your own writing, you must express your thoughts in clear, coherent sentences that produce precisely the reader response you want. Effective sentences are similar to the threads in a piece of knitting or weaving. If any sentence is fuzzy or obscure, the reader may lose the point of your discussion and in some cases never bother to regain it. Therefore, to retain your readers, you must concentrate on writing informative, effective sentences that continuously clarify the purpose of your essay.

Many problems in sentence clarity involve errors in grammar, punctuation, word choice, and usage. In this unit you'll find some general suggestions for writing clear, concise, engaging sentences. Your readers only read the words on the page, not those in your mind—so it's up to you to make sure the sentences in your essay express the thoughts in your head as closely and vividly as possible.

Developing a Clear Style

When you are ready to revise the sentences in your rough draft for clarity, consider the following rules:

1. Give Your Sentences Content

Fuzzy sentences are often the result of fuzzy thinking. Don't pad your paragraphs with sentences that run in circles, leading nowhere; rethink your ideas and revise your writing so that every sentence contributes to the construction of a solid discussion. In other words, commit yourself to a position and make each sentence contain information pertinent to your point.

Sometimes, however, you may have a definite idea in mind but still continue to write statements that alone do not contain enough information to make a specific point in your discussion. Frequently, an empty sentence can be revised by combining with the sentence that follows, as shown in the examples below. The empty or overly general sentences are underlined.

Poor: There are many kinds of beautiful tropical fish. The most popular kind with aquarium owners is the angelfish.

Better: Of the many kinds of beautiful tropical fish, the angelfish is the most popular with aquarium owners.

Poor: D. W. Griffith introduced many new cinematic techniques. Some of these techniques were contrast editing, close-ups, fade-outs, and freeze-frame shots.

Better: D. W. Griffith made movie history by introducing such new cinematic techniques as contrast editing, close-ups, fade-outs, and the freeze-frame shot.

Poor: There is a national organization called The Couch Potatoes. The group's 8,000 members are devoted television watchers.

Better: The Couch Potatoes is a national organization whose 8,000 members are devoted television watchers.

2. Make Your Sentences Specific

In addition to containing an informative, complete thought, each of your sentences should give readers enough clear details to "see" the picture you are creating. Clear, specific details are the only sure way to attract and hold the reader's interest. Therefore, make each sentence contribute something new and interesting to the overall discussion.

The following examples first show sentences that are far too vague to sustain any attention. After rewriting, these sentences contain specific details that add clarity and interest:

Vague: She went home in a bad mood.

Specific: She stomped home, hands jammed in her pockets, angrily kicking rocks, dogs, small children, and anything else that crossed her path.

Vague: His neighbor bought a really nice old desk.

Specific: His neighbor bought an oak roll-top desk made in 1885 that contains a secret drawer triggered by a hidden spring.

Vague: My roommate is truly horrible.

Specific: My thoughtless roommate leaves dirty dishes under the bed, sweaty clothes in the closet, and toenail clippings in the sink.

3. Avoid Mixed Constructions and Faulty Predication

Sometimes you may begin with a sentence pattern in mind and then shift to another pattern—a change that often results in a generally confusing sentence. In many of these cases, you will find that the subject of your sentence simply doesn't fit with the rest of the sentence (the predicate). Look at the following examples and note their corrections:

Faulty: Financial aid is a growing problem for many college students. [Financial aid itself isn't a problem; rather, it's the lack of aid.]

Revised: College students are finding it harder to obtain financial aid.

Faulty: Love is when you start rehearsing dinner-date conversation before breakfast. [A thing is never a "when" or a "where"; rewrite all "is when" or "is where" constructions.]

Revised: You're in love if you start rehearsing dinner-date conversation before breakfast.

Faulty: My math grade is why I'm so depressed. [A grade is not a "why"; rewrite "is why" constructions.]

Revised: I'm so depressed because of my math grade.

Many mixed constructions occur when a writer is in a hurry; read your rough drafts carefully to see if you have sentences in which you started one pattern but switched to another.

Developing a Lively Style

Good writing demands clarity and conciseness—but that's not all. Good prose must also be lively, engaging, and interesting. It should excite, intrigue, and charm the reader; each line should seduce the reader into the next. An article may be written clearly, but perhaps it failed to interest or inform.

You can prevent your readers from losing interests by developing a vigorous prose style that continually surprises and pleases them. As you revise your rough drafts, remember: bored readers are not born but made. Therefore, here are some practical suggestions to help you write lively sentences and paragraphs:

1. Use specific, descriptive verbs

Avoid bland verbs that must be supplemented by modifiers.

Bland: His fist broke the window into many small pieces.

Better: His fist shattered the window.

Bland: Dr. Love asked his congregation about donating money to his "love mission" over and over again.

Better: Dr. Love hounded his congregation into donating money to his "love mission".

Bland: The exhausted runner went up the last hill in an unsteady way.

Better: The exhausted runner staggered up the last hill.

2. Use specific, precise modifiers that help the reader see, hear, or feel what you are describing

Adjectives such as "good", "bad", "many", "more", "great", "a lot", "important", and "interesting" are too vague to paint the reader a clear picture. Similarly, the adverbs "very", "really", "too" and "quite" are overused and add little clarity to sentences. The following are examples of weak sentences and their revisions:

Imprecise: The potion changed the scientist into a really old man.

Better: The potion changed the scientist into a one-hundred-year-old man.

Imprecise: Aricelli is a very interesting person.

Better: Aricelli is witty, intelligent, and talented.

Imprecise: The vegetables tasted funny.

Better: The vegetables tasted like moss mixed with Krazy Glue.

3. Emphasize people when possible

Try to focus on human beings rather than abstractions whenever you can. Next to our fascinating selves, we most enjoy hearing about other people. Although all the sentences in the first paragraph that follows are correct, the revised one is clearer and more useful because the jargon has been eliminated and the focus has changed from the tuition rules to the students.

Original: Tuition regulations currently in effect provide that payment of the annual tuition entitles an undergraduate-degree candidate to full-time enrollment, which is defined as registration for three, four, or five courses per semester. This means that at no time may an undergraduate student's official registration for courses drop below three without a dean's permission for part-time status and that at no time may the official course registration exceed five. (Brown University Course Announcement)

Revised: If students pay their tuition, they may enroll in three, four, or five courses per semester. Fewer than three or more than five can be taken only with a dean's permission.

Obviously, the revised sentence is the more easily understood between the two because the reader knows exactly who will be affected by the pay cuts. In your own prose, wherever appropriate, try to replace vague abstractions, such as "society", "culture", "administrative concerns", and "programmatic expectations", with the human beings you're thinking about. In other words, remember to talk to people about people.

4. Vary your sentence style

Don't force readers to read through annoying paragraphs full of identically constructed sentences. To illustrate this point, the following are a few sentences composed in the all-too-common "subject + predicate" pattern:

Soccer is the most popular sport in the world. Soccer exists in almost every country. Soccer players are sometimes more famous than movie stars. Soccer teams compete every few years for the World Soccer Cup. Soccer fans often riot if their team loses. Soccer fans even commit suicide. Soccer is the only game in the world that makes people so crazy.

Each of us tends to repeat a particular sentence pattern (though the choppy "subject+predicate" is by far the most popular). To avoid overdosing your readers with the same pattern, vary the length, arrangement, and complexity of your sentences.

5. Don't change your point of view between or within sentences

If, for example, you begin your essay discussing students as "they", don't switch midway—or midsentence—to "we" or "you".

Inconsistent: Students pay tuition, which should entitle them to some voice in the university's administration. Therefore, we deserve one student on the Board of Regents.

Consistent: Students pay tuition, which should entitle them to some voice in the university's administration. Therefore, they deserve one student on the Board of Regents.

Inconsistent: I like my photography class because we learn how to restore our old photos and how to take better color portraits of your family.

Consistent: I like my photography class because I'm learning how to restore my old photos and how to take better color portraits of my family.

Developing an Emphatic Style

Some words and phrases in your sentences are more important than others and therefore need more emphasis. Three ways to vary emphasis are by (1) word order, (2) coordination, and (3) subordination.

1. Word Order

The arrangement of words in a sentence can determine which idea receives the most emphasis. To stress a word or phrase, place it at the beginning of the sentence or at the end of the sentence. Accordingly, a word or phrase receives least emphasis when buried in the middle of the sentence. Compare the following examples, in which the word "murder" receives varying degrees of emphasis:

Least emphatic: For Colonel Mustard murder was the only solution.

Emphatic: Murder was Colonel Mustard's only solution.

Most emphatic: Colonel Mustard knew only one solution: murder.

Another use of word order to vary emphasis is inversion, taking a word out of its natural or usual position in a sentence and relocating it in an unexpected place.

Usual order: Parents who give their children both roots and wings are wise.

Inverted order: Wise are the parents who give their children both roots and wings.

Not all your sentences will contain words that need special emphasis. Good writing generally contains a mix of some sentences in natural order and others rearranged for special effects.

2. Coordination

When you want to stress two closely related ideas equally, coordinate them. In coordination, you join two sentences with a coordinating conjunction. To remember the coordinating conjunctions ("for", "and", "nor", "but", "or", "yet", "so"), think of the acronym FANBOYS; then always join two sentences with a comma and one of the FANBOYS. Here are two samples:

Choppy: Imelda brought home a pair of ruby slippers.
  Ferdinand made her return them.

Coordinated: Imelda brought home a pair of ruby slippers, but Ferdinand made her return them.

You can use coordination to show a relationship between ideas and to add variety to your sentence structures. Be careful, however, to select the right words while linking ideas. Sometimes when the writers are in a hurry, they join ideas that are clearly related in their own minds but whose relationship is confusing to the reader:

Confusing: My laboratory report isn't finished, and today my sister is leaving for a visit home.

Clear: I'm still working on my laboratory report, so I won't be able to catch a ride home with my sister who's leaving today.

You should also avoid using coordinating conjunctions to string too many ideas together like linked sausages:

Poor: We went inside the famous cave and the guide turned off the lights and we saw the rocks that glowed.

Revised: After we went inside the famous cave, the guide turned off the lights so we could see the rocks that glowed.

3. Subordination

Some sentences contain one main statement and one or more less emphasized elements; the less important ideas are subordinate to, or are dependent on, the sentence's main idea. Subordinating conjunctions introducing dependent clauses show a variety of relationships between the clauses and the main part of the sentence. Here are some examples of choppy, weak sentences and their revisions, which contain subordinate clauses:

Choppy: Lew makes bagels on Tuesday. Lines in front of his store are a block long.

Revised: When Lew makes bagels on Tuesday, lines in front of his store are a block long.

Effective use of subordination is one of the marks of a sophisticated writer because it presents adequate information in one smooth flow. Subordination, like coordination, also adds variety to your sentence construction.

Generally, when you subordinate one idea, you emphasize another, and put your important idea in the main clause. Also, don't let your most important idea become buried under an avalanche of subordinate clauses, as in the sentence that follows:

When he was told by his boss, who had always treated him fairly, that he was being fired from a job that he had held for twenty years at a factory where he enjoyed working because the pay was good, Henry felt angry and frustrated.

Exercises

I. In this exercise, you will find sentences that contain some of the problems discussed thus far in this chapter. Rewrite any sentences that you find vague, confusing, overly simplistic, or overpacked. You may divide or combine sentences and replace vague words to improve clarity.

1. There's a new detective show on television. Starring Phil Noir. It is set in the 1940s. According to *TV Guide*.

2. Roger was an awesome guy he was really a big deal in his company.

3. I can't help but wonder whether or not he isn't unwelcome.

4. The book Biofeedback: How to Stop. It is a good book because of all the good ideas the writer put into it.

5. His assistant stole the magician's bag of tricks. The magician became disillusioned.

6. Afraid poor repair service will ruin your next road trip? Come to the Fix-It Shop and be sure. If your car has a worn-out part, we'll replace it with one just like it.

7. I've signed up for a course at my local college, it is "Cultivating the Mold in Your Refrigerator for Fun and Profit".

8. For some people, reading your horoscope is a fun way to learn stuff about your life. Although some people think it's too weird.

II. Replace the following underlined words so that the sentences are clear and vivid. In addition, rephrase any awkward constructions or unnecessarily abstract words you find.

1. Judging from the <u>crazy</u> sound of the reactor, it isn't obvious to me that nuclear power as we know it today isn't a technology with a less than wonderful future.

2. The City Council felt <u>bad</u> because the revised tourist development activities grant fund application form letters were mailed without stamps.

3. To watch Jim Bob eat pork chops was <u>most interesting</u>.

4. For sale: <u>very nice</u> antique bureau suitable for ladies or gentlemen with thick legs and extra-large side handles.

5. We <u>don't want anybody to not</u> have fun.

6. My roommate is <u>sort of different</u>, but he's a good guy at heart.

7. After reading the great new book, The Looter's Guide to Riot-Prone Cities, Eddie <u>asked to have</u> a transfer really soon.

8. The wild oats soup was <u>fantastic</u>, so we drank a lot of it very fast.

9. When his new cat Chairman Meow won the pet show, owner Warren Peace got <u>pretty excited</u>.

10. The new diet <u>made me feel awful</u>, and it did many horrible things to my body.

III. Combine the following simple sentences into one complex sentence.

1. Norman Bates manages a motel. It is remote.

   It is dangerous.

   Norman has a mother.

   She seems overly fond of knives. He tries to protect his mom.

2. A showman goes to the jungle.

   He captures an ape.

   The ape is a giant.

   The ape is taken to New York City. He escapes.

   He dies fighting for a young woman. He loves her.

   She is beautiful.

3. Rick is an American. He is cynical.

   He owns a café.

   He lives in Casablanca. He meets his former love. She is married.

   Her husband is a French resistance fighter. Rick helps the couple.

   He regains self-respect.

IV. The following two paragraphs are poorly written because of their choppy, wordy, and monotonous sentences. Rewrite each paragraph so that it is clear, lively, and emphatic.

1. There is a new invention on the market. It is called a "dieter's conscience". It is a small box to be installed in one's refrigerator. When the door of the refrigerator is opened by you, a tape recorder begins to start. A really loud voice yells, "You eating again? No wonder you're getting fat." Then the very loud voice says, "Close the door; it's getting warm." Then the voice laughs a lot in an insane and crazy fashion. The idea is one that is designed to mock

people into a habit of stopping eating.

2. In this modern world of today, man has come up with another new invention. This invention is called the "Talking Tombstone". It is made by the Gone-But-Not-Forgotten Company, which is located in Burbank, California. This company makes a tombstone that has a device in it that makes the tombstone appear to be talking aloud in a realistic fashion when people go close by it. The reason is that the device is really a recording machine that is turned on due to the simple fact of the heat of the bodies of the people who go by. The closer the people get, the louder the sound the tombstone makes. It is this device that individual persons who want to leave messages after death may utilize. A hypochondriac, to cite one example, might leave a recording of a message that says over and over again in a really loud voice, "See, I told you I was sick!" It may be assumed by one and all that this new invention will be a serious aspect of the whole death situation in the foreseeable future.

Paragraph Development

A paragraph is a series of sentences all relating to the same topic or central idea. The aim of all paragraphs is to communicate to the reader that idea clearly and effectively. There is no hard and fast rule about the length of a paragraph; it depends on the topic and what the writer wants to say. The paragraph should be long enough to develop the idea expressed in the topic sentence sufficiently. It should do what it sets out to do in the topic sentence. Regardless of the length, the paragraph must contain only one idea. Any irrelevant sentences must be eliminated from the paragraph to ensure its unity.

I. Parts of the Paragraph

There are three parts in a paragraph: a topic sentence, supporting sentences, and a conclusion. The first and last sentences are general statements about the topic, which tie the paragraph together. The middle sentences contain information, facts, opinions, and examples that support or develop the topic sentence.

1. Topic Sentence

The topic sentence is usually the first sentence in the paragraph and limits the topic of the paragraph. The topic sentence is always a complete thought or sentence. Most words in the title are capitalized. Only the first word and proper nouns are capitalized in the topic sentence. The most important sentence of a paragraph is the topic sentence because it contains the main ideas of the paragraph. There are three elements in a topic sentence: the topic, a controlling idea, and the point of view of the writer.

1) *Topic*

The topic is the subject, that is, what is being written about in the paragraph. The main idea expressed in the topic sentence should not be too general or too specific. If it is too general, it will be difficult to develop in a single paragraph adequately. If it is too specific, there will be nothing left to say to develop the idea in the paragraph. Look at the following topic sentences:

Everyone can benefit from exercise. *

This topic sentence is too general. Different kinds of exercise have different benefits. Not all of them can be developed within one paragraph.

Doing aerobics for thirty minutes a day will strengthen a person's cardiovascular system by twenty five percent. *

This topic sentence is too specific. There is nothing else that can be said to support this statement in the rest of the paragraph.

There are three reasons why I exercise every day.

This sentence is an adequate topic sentence. It limits the discussion of the paragraph to only discussing the reasons that the writer exercises. Telling what those three reasons are and what benefits the writer gains from exercise can be expanded upon in the paragraph.

2) *Controlling Idea*

The controlling idea limits the topic of the paragraph to one definite idea or one aspect of the topic that represents a particular idea, feeling, or opinion. The controlling idea must not be too broad, it must be specific enough for the subject to be discussed within one paragraph. Look at these three topic sentences (as shown in Table 2-1). Each has the same topic but contains different controlling ideas.

Table 2-1

Topic	Controlling Idea
The Grand Canyon	is noted for its inspiring panorama. (controlling idea: panorama)
The Grand Canyon	is a favorite vacation spot for travelers worldwide. (controlling idea: vacation spot)
The Grand Canyon	is an ideal area to view the geologic history of the earth. (controlling idea: geologic history)

A divided topic sentence is useful in ensuring the sentence has a controlling idea. In a divided topic sentence, the writer specifies or explains the divisions of the topic. Look at the following sentences that illustrate a divided topic sentence:

There are **three** major professional sports in America.

Five essential ingredients are required in learning a foreign language.

To become successful, a writer needs **four** basic skills.

All the three divided topic sentences above clearly limit what will be discussed in the paragraph (three sports, five ingredients, and four skills).

3) *Point of View*

A good topic sentence also expresses the point of view of the writer. It may contain the opinion or attitude of the writer. In the following topic sentence:

Digital cameras make photography easy and fun.

The writer's point of view is easily determined—it's easy and fun.

Compare with *Steven King has written many books.*

In this statement, the writer's opinion of the works of Steven King is not evident, nor is there any indication of whether being such a writer is good or bad.

2. Supporting Sentences

The topic sentence is usually fairly general. The supporting sentences that follow it should be more specific and develop the idea expressed in the topic sentence. There are several methods that can be employed to make the supporting sentences more specific. One is to use details, facts, statistics, examples, opinions, research results, personal experience, or anecdotes. For example:

Seoul is a big city. (no statistics, just a broad statement)

Seoul from South Korea has a population of over 10 million people.

Another method of adding specificity is by using exact names of things rather than writing about them in general terms. For example:

He is a doctor. (a very general statement)

He is a pediatrician who has worked at City Hospital for the last 15 years. (a very specific statement)

The final method is to use concrete words that allow the readers to imagine the topic being written about in greater detail, and not just in general or abstract terms. For example:

Mr. Thompson enjoys life.

Mr. Thompson is almost always in a good mood, most often has a smile on his face, is quick to laugh, and always sees the positive side even in terrible situations.

Look at the following paragraph and note the supporting sentences.

(1) The invention of the automobile has provided many benefits to travelers. (2) With a car, travelers are able to travel vast distances in short periods of time. What once took two or three weeks on horseback or horse drawn wagon can now be done in a matter of hours. (3) The comfort enjoyed by travelers, compared to a horse drawn wagon, is amazing. No longer do travelers have to endure the bone-jarring ordeal of riding on a	(1) Topic sentence (2) Supporting 1: Speed (3) Supporting 2: Comfort

stiff leather saddle or splinter-infested wagon seat. Their voyage is now made on softly cushioned seats that can be adjusted to fit the sojourners' level of comfort. (4) Travelers are no longer subjected to the harsh elements of the weather. In the past, travelers had to suffer the biting cold of winter and the blistering heat of summer, not to mention the suffering encountered by gale force winds, blinding snow, and drenching rain. Today people can enjoy a soothing and relaxing trip thanks to the totally enclosed interiors that offer air conditioning and heating units in most vehicles. (5) Needless to say, with all the advantages an automobile has to offer, no one would dream of using the expression "Get a horse" today.	(4) Supporting 3: Controlled Environment (5) Conclusion

3. Concluding Sentence

The concluding sentence is the last sentence of the paragraph. Single paragraph compositions should have a concluding sentence; however, it may not be necessary all the time for a multi-paragraph composition. The function of the concluding sentence is to signal the end of the paragraph. Concluding sentences can either be a restatement of the topic sentence, a summary of the supporting sentences, or contain a final comment about the topic. The concluding sentence in a paragraph should be a general statement that relates to the idea expressed in the topic sentence, and not another fact or detail of support. If restating the topic sentence, it should be expressed in different words, not an exact copy of the topic sentence.

In the above paragraph about automobiles, the concluding sentence was a final comment about automobiles. A concluding sentence that restates the topic sentence could be "The examples mentioned above clearly demonstrate the many advantages of the automobile". A concluding sentence that summarizes the supporting sentences could be "Speed, comfort, and a controlled environment are just a few of the advantages that a modern-day car has over a horse".

Many words or phrases can be used to signal the end of the paragraph in the concluding sentence. Here are just a few:

finally, in conclusion, therefore, indeed, thus, in brief, in summary, as a result, in short ...

Other phrases include:

we can see that ...

it is clear that ...

these examples show that ...

there can be no doubt that ...

the evidence suggests that ...

II. Paragraph Character

The information in each paragraph must adequately explain, exemplify, define, or in some other way support your topic sentence. Therefore, you must include enough supporting information or evidence in each paragraph to make your readers understand your topic sentence. Moreover, you must make the information in the paragraph clear and specific enough for the readers to accept your ideas. A well-written paragraph has four characteristics: unity, completeness, cohesion, and continuity.

1. Unity

Unity means discussing only one idea in the paragraph, which is presented in the topic sentence. If a sentence in the paragraph does not relate to the topic sentence, it is irrelevant and should be deleted.

Every sentence in a body paragraph should relate directly to the main idea presented by the topic sentence. A paragraph must stick to its announced subject; it must not drift away into another discussion. In other words, a good paragraph has unity.

Now look at the following paragraph, in which the writer strays from his original purpose:

(1) Cigarette smoke is unhealthy even for people who don't have the nicotine habit themselves. (2) Secondhand smoke can cause asthmatics and sufferers of sinusitis serious problems. (3) Doctors regularly advise heart patients to avoid confined smoky areas because coronary attacks might be triggered by the lack of clean air. (4) Moreover, having the smell of smoke in one's hair and clothes is a real nuisance. (5) Even if a person doesn't have any health problems, exhaled smoke doubles the amount of carbon monoxide in the air, which may cause the person lung problems in the future.	Sentence (4) shifts from the topic

Sentence 4 refers to smoke as a nuisance and therefore does not belong in the paragraph that discusses smoking as a health hazard to nonsmokers.

Sometimes a large portion of a paragraph will drift into another topic. In the following paragraph, did the writer wish to focus on her messiness or on the beneficial effects of her engagement?

I have always been a very messy person. As a child, I was a pack rat, saving every little piece of insignificant paper that I thought might be important when I grew up. As a teenager, I filled my pockets with remnants of basketball tickets, hall passes, gum wrappers, and other important articles from my high school education. As a college student, I became a "boxer"—not a fighter, but someone who cannot throw anything away and therefore it winds up in a box in my closet. *But my engagement has changed everything. I'm really pleased with the new stage of my life, and I owe it all to my fiancé. My overall outlook on life has changed because of his influence on me. I'm neater, much more cheerful, and I'm even getting places on time like I never did before. It's truly amazing what love can do.*	Shift from the topic of messiness

This writer may wish to discuss the changes her fiancé has brought her and then use her former messiness, tardiness, and other bad habits as examples to illustrate those changes; however, as presented here, the paragraph is not unified around a central idea. On the contrary, it first seems to promise a discussion of her messiness but then wanders into comments on "what love can do".

2. Completeness

Completeness is similar to unity, except that instead of including sentences that are irrelevant, completeness is ensuring that all the necessary supporting sentences are included to fully explain and support the topic.

For example, if a topic sentence states that three things are needed to obtain a visa and only two are mentioned in the supporting sentences, the paragraph is incomplete. All the three items must be mentioned for the paragraph to have completeness. Another example, if a topic sentence promises to list the steps needed to change a flat tire but neglects to mention that the car must be jacked up before taking off the wheels, the paragraph is incomplete. All the steps needed to change a tire must be included in the paragraph to ensure completeness.

3. Cohesion

Cohesion is the smooth, continuous flow of thoughts of the sentences and ideas presented according to some logical principle. Cohesion allows the reader to follow the flow of ideas within the text without effort, confusion, or frustration because all the sentences are connected together and sequenced in a rational order in their support of the topic sentence. If the supporting sentences in the paragraph are arranged without rational order, the paragraph must be lacking cohesiveness.

The principle used in ordering the sentences within a paragraph depends on the kind of paragraph being written. Chronological ordering is appropriate for narratives, which uses a time order of events to relate the sequence in which things happen. An example would be a paragraph about instructions for assembling a model airplane. A descriptive paragraph uses spatial ordering to ensure cohesion. In a descriptive paragraph, items could be described from left to right, top to bottom, front to back, etc. The principles of logic and reason are used in expository paragraphs, which arrange the sentences into a logical pattern.

To ensure cohesion, transition words are used to fill in the gaps between sentences in a paragraph. Usually transition words are at the beginning of a sentence to relate a sentence to the one preceding it, but transition words can come within sentences to connect one idea to another.

4. Continuity

Continuity is the combined inclusion of the three characteristics mentioned above: unity, completeness, and cohesion. Having all three characteristics in the paragraph ensures that the connection between ideas presented is smooth and even. To achieve continuity in a paragraph, it must have all three of these characteristics.

Exercises

I. Rewrite the following general statements and make them more specific and suitable as topic sentences.

1. Italian food is healthy and easy to prepare.
   _____

2. The United States government is over burdened with citizens' complaints.
   _____

3. Natural disasters create havoc for everyone.
   _____

4. The extinction of species of life on earth will have a profound effect on future generations.
   _____

5. Fairy tales are beneficial to children.
   _____

II. Identify the topic and controlling idea of the following topic sentences.

1. Children's educational programs on TV are superior to cartoons for young minds.
Topic: _____
Controlling idea: _____

2. Hobbies provide people with many benefits.

Topic: _____

Controlling idea: _____

3. Learning a foreign language is also about learning the culture of that country.

Topic: _____

Controlling idea: _____

III. Read the following paragraphs and write a topic sentence and a concluding sentence for each.

1. Topic sentence: _____

Acid rain is the result of pollutants, which are released into the atmosphere from automobiles and industry. It falls back to earth after being trapped by rain and snow. There have been numerous scientific studies of the effects of acid rain on the ecosystem in recent years. Pollutants contained in acid rain destroy plants and animals life when it enters lakes and rivers. Millions of acres of trees and plants have been damaged or destroyed because of the harmful effects of acid rain on these delicate ecosystems.

Concluding sentence: _____

2. Topic sentence: _____

It has only recently come under more intense investigation by proponents of western medical practices. Acupuncture involves the insertion of small needles, with the application of heat and electrical stimulation at precise acupuncture points on the body. According to traditional Chinese doctors, the balance of yin and yang (opposing forces that regulate spiritual, emotional, physical, and mental balance) are essential for good health. Blockage of the GI flow (the energy that flows through the body via meridians or pathways) creates an imbalance of yin and yang, which results in health problems or illness. The insertion of needles into the skin during acupuncture treatments unblock these channels and allow energy flows to optimizing, resulting in improved health.

Concluding sentence: _____

IV. The cohesiveness of the paragraph below could be improved with the addition of transition words. Insert the appropriate transition words from the list below in the blanks.

| undoubtedly | furthermore | as a result | in addition |
| whereas | although | following | nonetheless |

Tutankhamen, _____ not as notable a pharaoh as Seti I or Rameses II, _____ gained wide-spread fame because of his tomb. Howard Carter discovered

Tutankhamen's tomb in 1922 in the Valley of the Kings. Surprisingly, the tomb was largely intact; _____ most Egyptian tombs had been pillaged and plundered over the last 3000 years by grave robbers. The treasures revealed in the tomb include his mummy and solid gold sarcophagus. _____ a priceless gold mask, wall paintings, furniture, chariots, statues, jewelry items, weapons, games, clothing, cosmetic equipment, and other artifacts were discovered. _____, these items have given archeologists a unique portrait of the life of ancient Egyptian royalty. _____, to add to the tomb's myth, _____ the opening of the tomb a number of unexplained and mysterious deaths sparked rumors of the mummy's curse. _____, it was widely believed that anyone disturbing the peaceful remains of the tomb was doomed to a terrible death. Much more can be learned about the legend and treasures of Tutankhamen by visiting the Egyptian Museum in Cairo.

V. The sentences below are out of order. By noting the various transitional devices, arrange the sentences into a coherent paragraph.

How to Purchase a New Car

a If you're happy with the car's performance, find out about available financing arrangements.

b Later, at home, study your notes carefully to help you decide which car fits your needs.

c After you have discussed various loans and interest rates, you can negotiate the final price with the salesperson.

d A visit to the showroom also allows you to test drive the car.

e Once you have agreed on the car's price, feel confident that you have made a well-chosen purchase.

f Next, a visit to a nearby showroom should help you select the color, options, and style of the car.

g First, take a trip to the library to read the current auto magazines and consumers' guides.

h As you read, take notes on models and prices.

VI. Rearrange the sentences below which lack a degree of cohesion in a correct sequential order to form a logical paragraph. Rewrite and use the cohesive devices to make a well written paragraph.

a The Hope Diamond's unparalleled beauty and uniqueness is attributed to the diamond's unquestioned perfection, large size, and brilliant blue color.

b The Hope Diamond, one of the world's great treasures, has been enshrouded in

tragedy and mystery for centuries.
c   Her first son died in a car accident at age 9.
d   Death has followed its history.
e   It is alleged that Tavernier stole the Hope Diamond from the stature of a Hindu goddess and was mauled by a pack of wild dogs after selling the stone in Russia.
f   Whether the legend of the Hope Diamond is believed or not, thousands still marvel at its beauty and are allured daily by the museum's display.
g   The next owner, a New York jeweler named Harry Winston, donated the gem to the Smithsonian Institute in 1958.
h   In 1939, the diamond was purchased by Henry Philip Hope (from which the gem gets its current name).
i   According to the legend, Hope went bankrupt because of the curse.
j   She considered the gem a good luck charm: however, tragedy struck her life after the purchase.
k   The curse began with a traveler to India named Tavernier.
l   Her daughter committed suicide at the age of 25.
m   Her husband was committed to a mental institution for insanity and remained there until his death.
n   Many believe that the donation was made in order to rid himself of the diamond's curse.
o   Some attribute the beheading of Marie Antoinette and Louis XVI, later owners of the famous diamond, to the curse of the Hope Diamond.
p   An American woman, Evelyn Walsh McLean, bought the diamond in 1910.

Social Letters

Letters are well-organized in form and content, generally follow a pattern that is similar to basic composition writing. A well-composed letter, like a good composition in English, usually has three basic components:

1. A salutation, corresponding to the introduction;
2. A general message, corresponding to the body;
3. A closing and signature, corresponding to the conclusion.

There are two kinds of letters which we most likely encounter: social letters and business letters. For both types, indeed for almost any letter written in English, there is a general layout that is followed and several general components that are required. The following model sets out (1) the writer's address, (2) the salutation to the addressee, (3) the body of message, (4) the closing word or phrase, and (5) the writer's signature.

MODEL LETTER

```
                                                writer's city/state/zip code
                                                writer's country
                                                month/day/year
    salutation(Dear)+addressee's name
    Body of the letter
    _____
    _____
    _____
    _____
                                                closing,
                                                (writer's name)
```

1. Writer's Address

Although you will usually find that the writer places his/her address in the upper right-hand corner of the page, business correspondents may place their addresses in the letterhead at the middle top of the page, or at the lower left-hand corner.

2. Envelope Address

On the envelope, the U.S. post office requires the addressee's name on the first line, the street address on the second line, the city/state/zip code on the third line, and the name of the country on the last line. All of this should appear in the center of the envelope. The writer's name and address should appear in the upper left-hand corner of the envelope.

MODEL ENVELOPE

write's full name	
writer's street address	STAMP
writer's city/state/zip code	
writer's country	
(title)addressee's full name	
addressee's street address	
addressee's city/state/zip code	
addressee's country	

3. Salutation

Salutations are placed on the left margin. As a general rule, when the writer knows the addressee well and is on a "first name" basis, the writer begins an informal social letter with "Dear" followed by the addressee's first or given name:

Example: Dear John, Dear Mary, etc.

For formal social letters and business letters, however, the salutation "Dear" is followed by the addressee's title and family name:

Example: Dear Mr. Smithson, Dear Dr, Jones, etc.

In business letter salutations, the reader may also note other forms, for example: Dear Publisher, Dear Editor, Dear Reader, Dear Parents, Dear Colleague, etc. This avoids the use of Dear Sir and Gentlemen, which are now outdated as they assume all readers are male and overlook the growing number of women in the business world.

In business letters, the reader may also note the use of Ms., which is the exact linguistic equivalent of Mr.; that is, Ms. indicates female gender but not whether the person is married.

4. Body of the Letter

The letter itself may also begin exactly on the left margin, directly under the salutation, or it may be indented five spaces from the left, the traditional signal for a new paragraph in English. If you prefer not to indent for each new paragraph, you should leave an extra space between paragraphs.

A formal or business letter usually includes the following parts: (1) introduce him/herself (2) state the purpose of the letter, and (3) conclude the letter.

5. Closing Signature

The closing and signature at the end of the letter are usually spaced from the right margin and aligned under the address and date that appear in the upper right-hand corner. If there is any possibility that the person receiving your letter may not be able to read your signature, you should carefully print or type your name under your handwritten signature.

Remember that when the reader answers your letter and addresses the envelope, he/she must be able to spell your name clearly and correctly. Your letter is the only guideline to spell your name and address correctly.

In summary, a good letter must be clearly thought out and organized on paper. Its message should be understandable to the reader and its appearance on the page should be well-balanced, like a picture in a frame. A letter carries the writer's unspoken thoughts and silently reflects the writer's personality.

Invitations

Overview

An invitation is a request to attend an event. All major and many minor life events are possible occasions in which we invite people. It could be a formal invitation to banquets, lunches, cocktail parties, receptions, to conduct business, to improve employee morale, and to solidify relationships with clients, customers, suppliers, and others. Or it could be an informal invitation to a barbecue, a night at the theater, your child's violin recital, a birthday or anniversary party, a housewarming, to name just a few possibilities. It could be for a formal event or a casual one, even a religious event.

Formal invitations are engraved or printed on fine-quality note paper, use a line-by-line style, and are phrased in the third person. Each invited person is mentioned by name and honorific (Ms., Mrs., Miss, Dr., Mr.) either on the envelope or in the invitation itself. Abbreviations are not used.

Informal social invitations use either commercial fill-in cards or are handwritten on informal stationery in usual letter style. Informal business invitations may be sent on letterhead stationery; in-house invitations may be issued via memo, even sometimes by e-mail.

Format

- State the occasion.
- Give the date and time.
- Give the address.
- Invitation followed by an address or phone number. If appropriate, give a date by which you need a response.

- Indicate the preferred dress in the lower right corner, when appropriate.
- Additional information might include parking facilities, alternate arrangements in case of rain, and an offer of transportation.
- Express your anticipated pleasure in seeing the person.

Models

Formal Invitation
Model 1

Rita Smith	*Salutation*
requests the pleasure of your company	*Invitation*
at	
The Grand Opening Celebration	*Event*
of	
The Gathering Together	
Sunday, the 9th of November, 2023	*Time*
from	
three o'clock until seven o'clock in the evening	
202 N. Elm St.	*Address*
Locust Valley, IN	

Model 2

Professor Li Xing School of Foreign Languages and Literatures Wuhan University	*Title of addressee*
Dear Sir,	*Salutation*
It is a great pleasure for us to invite you to speak at the opening session of our annual seminar on translation theories to be held at our university on July 5 at 9:00 a.m.	*Invitation* *Time & Address*
As the translation theory master, you have the global reputation and own the important position in the translation field. So we sincerely invite you here to strengthen the academic exchange between our two universities.	*Reason of the occasion*
We would appreciate having your reply by July 3 so that we can finalize our program.	*Date of response*
Sincerely, College of Foreign Languages of USST	*Closing*

Model 3

Dear Sir/Madam, We hereby sincerely invite you and your company representatives to participate in one of the BMC Global IT Management Activities, BMC Exchange, at Langham Hotel, Shanghai, on April 22, 2023. In the BMC Exchange Shanghai, we will offer hot topics, put forward solutions and demonstrate case analyses in IT management in various fields. It will be a great pleasure to meet you at the exchange. We hope to establish a long-term business relationship with your company in the future. Yours sincerely, Chen Meng General Manager	*Invitation* *Time & Address* *State the occasion* *Pleasure in seeing the person* *Closing signature*

Model 4

Dear Sir/Madam, Information safety has become a problematic issue for many companies in the information era. Our company is holding an exhibition to provide solutions for customers from various fields. The exhibition will be on May 19, from 10:00 a.m. to 4:00 p.m., at City Exhibition Centre. We sincerely hope you will attend the exhibition and acquire sound solutions for your company. Faithfully yours, Skyline Co. Ltd.	*Reasons* *Invitation* *Time & Address* *Pleasure in seeing the person* *Closing*

Informal Invitation

Model 5

TO: Jeffrey Cohen WHAT: Stephen's 10th birthday party WHEN: Saturday, October 9, 3 p.m.–5 p.m. WHERE: Sport World Amusements, 345 Arcadia Road, Anytown, USA Games Rides Laser tag	*Basic information* *Invitation in casual style*

Indoor mini golf Pizza and soft drinks+ Birthday cake+ For parents, too! Casual dress — wear something comfortable! R.S.V.P.! 555-5555	*No closing signature*

Model 6

Dear Dr. and Mrs. Davidson,
    We will be celebrating Paula and Steve's thirtieth year of ministry with a dinner at the Florida Commons Restaurant, Saturday, November 29th, at 8:00 p.m. Please let us know by Monday the 24th if you can join us on this happy occasion.
                                               With love,
                                               (writer's name)
	Casual style to tell the information of the invitation

Useful Vocabulary and Expressions

Words

attend	cancel	celebrate	commemorate
debut	festival	honor	installation
occasion	pleasure	salute	R.S.V. P

Phrases

accept with pleasure	be our guest
have the honor of inviting	cordially invites you to
in honor of	in commemoration/celebration of
kindly respond on or before	invite you to
obliged to recall/cancel/postpone	looking forward to seeing you
request the pleasure of your company	owing to the illness/death of

Sentences

- I'm pleased to invite you to ...
- Are you free after work on Friday to join a few of us for dinner?
- Come hear noted Reformation scholar and professor of history Dr. Margaret Heath speak on September 12 at the 8:30 and 11:00 services at Gloria Dei Lutheran Church, 1924 Forster Avenue.
- Horseback riding will be available, dress accordingly.
- It will be so good to see you.
- Mr. and Mrs. Faraday regret that it is necessary to cancel their invitation to brunch on

Sunday, the sixteenth of August, because of the illness of their daughter.
- Please confirm by June 6 that you can attend.
- Please join us for a farewell party in honor of Veronica Roderick, who is leaving to pursue other business interests.
- You are invited to a special evening show of our new line of furniture from European designers.

Exercises

I. Read the following Invitation and match each part with a short description of what the writer is doing.

A.

	In this part, the writer:
Haidée Czelovar Power and Raoul Czelovar cordially invite you to a reception celebrating the	1._____
Golden Wedding Anniversary of	2._____
Simone Rakonitz Czelovar and Karl Czelovar	
Sunday, the second of April	3._____
at eight o'clock	
Wyatt's Village Inn	4._____
Indianapolis	
R.S.V. P. Formal Dress	5._____

B.

	In this part, the writer:
Dear Sir/Madam,	
Information safety has become a problematic issue for many companies in the information era. Our company is holding an exhibition to provide solutions for customers from various fields. The exhibition will be on May 19, from 10:00 a.m. to 4:00 p.m., at City Exhibition Centre.	1._____ 2._____ 3._____
We sincerely hope you will attend the exhibition and acquire sound solutions for your company.	4._____
Faithfully yours, Skyline Co., Ltd.	5._____

II. Write Invitations based on the information given in both formal and informal style.

Addresser: Li Guang, Marketing Manager

Addressee: Mr. Song

Occasion: Dinner party for 10th anniversary of TT Express
Time: 20:00, Oct.9
Place: Garden Hotel in Hangzhou

Formal Invitation
_____
_____
_____
_____

Informal Invitation
_____
_____
_____
_____

Thank-you Letters

Overview

In our fast-paced society, the polite act of writing thank-you letters has become increasingly rare. Many people prefer to thank people with a quick phone call or text message, rather than take the time to write and send a personal letter. The extra effort will be appreciated and make you stand out from the crowd.

Thank-you letters enhance business and personal relationships. Despite this, people find them difficult to write, which is perhaps why so many arrive late or not at all.

Even when you have graciously thanked someone in person, a written thank you is often expected or required or, at least, appreciated. In the business world, the thank-you note has become a must if you care about your career. "Anyone too busy to say thank you will get fewer and fewer chances to say it."

It's easier to find the words when you feel grateful than it is after your enthusiasm has cooled. So, write soon. A wide variety of occasions are appropriate for sending thank-you letters. The most obvious is when you have received a gift. You should also thank people for favors, friendship, and effort expended on your behalf.

Format
- Express your gratitude in an enthusiastic, appreciative way.
- Describe in details what you are grateful for.
- Elaborate on your appreciation. Tell how useful or appropriate it is, how you plan to use it, where you have placed it, or how it enhances your life, home, office, wardrobe. Be specific about what pleased you.

- Close with one or two sentences of your gratitude again, with a few words unrelated to the object (expressing affection, promising to see the person soon, sending greetings to family members, saying something nice about the donor).

Models

Model 1

Dear Mr. Wu, I want to thank you for sending me the address and phone number of the gift shop in Hong Kong.	*First Thank You*
I called them this evening to ask about the tablecloths you told me about. You were right. They were most cordial and reasonable in their prices. I was able to order 10 tablecloths at a fraction of what they would have cost here in the States.	*Explanation*
Thank you once again for your kind gesture. <div style="text-align:right">Sincerely, Jan Robinson</div>	*Second Thank You*

Model 2

Dear Bob, In this busy world, it's gratifying when people take time to help others. It's the reason why I'm writing to thank you.	*First Thank You*
At your suggestion, Paul Kamak recently called to contract my services. I really appreciate this referral. It looks like Paul and I will be doing a lot of business in the future. I'm sure he will be pleased with my work and will be happy you offered my name.	*Explanation (implying that you will not make correspondent regret thinking of you)*
Thanks again for thinking of me. <div style="text-align:right">Warm regards, Jennifer Linde</div>	*Second Thank You*

Model 3

Dear Jennifer,	*First Thank You*
Just a quick note to thank you. I spoke to Jed Hasslen today. He told me that on my recommendation you hired him to make some illustrations for your customer newsletter. I'm glad to bring new business to a talented, young artist like Jed, and	*Explanation (assure the recipient that he or she won't regret helping you out.)*

I appreciate that you've given him a chance. I'm sure you'll be well pleased.
 	
    If there's ever anything I can do for you to return the favor, don't hesitate to ask. Thanks again!
 	
                                    Sincerely,
                                  Thomas Harvey
	Offer to return the favor at any time

Model 4

Dear Millicent,
 	
    The dinner party was elegant and memorable, and we were delighted to be included. I don't know anyone who has as much flair and style as you do when it comes to entertaining!
 	
                                  With much love
	Informal Thank-you letter

Useful Vocabulary and Expressions

Words

appreciate	gracious	generosity	superb	wonderful
charming	invaluable	timely	thrilled	remarkable
cherished	fascinated	memorable	luxurious	spectacular
delighted	grateful	perfect	over-whelmed	surprised
elegant	hospitable	sensational	satisfying	timeless
enchanted	flattered	overjoyed	well-made	unique
enjoyed	impressed	priceless	tasteful	

Phrases

really appreciate your help	appreciate your interest/kind words/referral
convey my personal thanks to everyone	
derived great pleasure from	cannot tell you how delighted I was
excellent/splendid suggestion	generous gift
from the bottom of my heart	how much it meant to us
heartfelt/hearty thanks	I have seldom seen such
I am indebted/very much obliged to you	it was hospitable/kind of you to made us feel so welcome
I'll long remember	
please accept my gratitude/our sincere appreciation	meant a great deal to me
profoundly touched by	very special occasion
we want you to know how much we value	we were especially pleased because
we were thrilled/delighted/stunned with	what a joy it was to receive

	your gift meant a lot to me at this time because

Sentences

- I appreciate your advice more than I can say.
- I can't remember when I've had a better/more pleasant/more relaxing/more enjoyable time.
- I can't thank you enough for ...
- I'm grateful for your help, and hope that I can reciprocate some day.
- I appreciate your concern very much.
- On behalf of ..., I thank you for your kind expression of sympathy.
- Special thanks to the doctors and the nurses at ... hospital.
- Thanks a million.
- Thank you for including me in this memorable/special event.
- Thank you for opening a charge account with us recently.
- Thank you for your courtesy and patience in ...
- Thank you for your generous donation to ...; I appreciate your comforting gesture very much.
- Thank you for your kind hospitality last night; I have never felt less a stranger in a strange city.
- Thank you so much for agreeing to speak to our study club.
- This is just a note to thank you for ...
- We all thank you for the tickets to the science museum.
- We are thrilled with the ... you sent!

Exercises

I. Read the following Thank-you letters and match each part with a short description of what the writer is doing.

A.

Dear Sol, Your offer is very generous, and I accept it! Our town school has a severe shortage of computers per student. Especially my son's third-grade class. Your old Mac is the perfect solution. I can pick up the Mac from you at your convenience and deliver it myself to Jason's classroom.	In this part, the writer: 1_____ 2_____

I know you said you have a lot of used computers around, but that doesn't make the act any less generous or helpful. I am grateful. Let me know how I can return the favor. 　　　　　　　　　　　　　　Sincerely, 　　　　　　　　　　　　　(writer's name)	3._____

B.

Dear Agnes and Walter, 　　Thank you for the lovely silver piggy bank you gave Anabel. It's a classic, and I know she will treasure it all her life. In the meantime, it has a place of honor on her dresser, and we've gotten into the habit of putting our change into it at the end of the day. 　　Can you come by to see your new little grand-niece sometime next week? We're all feeling rested by now and would love to see you. Give me a call. 　　　　　　　　　　　　　　With much love, 　　　　　　　　　　　　　(writer's name)	In this part, the writer: 1_____ 2._____ 3._____

II. Write Thank-you letters based on the information given.

1. Thanks for the help in supporting a seminar.

_____
_____

2. Thanks for the gift book you gave to my son.

_____
_____

3. Thanks for the contribution of $200 to the Alumni Annual Giving Campaign.

_____
_____

Apologies

Overview

When you have had difficulty or a conflict with a person, a letter of apology can be effective in setting things right. Apologizing by letter permits the other person to accept your apology, without argument. Another advantage of letter writing is that you can take your time composing your thoughts, and the recipient can similarly take his/her time considering your message and deciding how to respond. A letter doesn't oblige them to respond immediately; there's time to absorb the message and decide how to react. Write as soon as possible. Procrastination turns writing an apology into a major effort and will exhaust your patience of writing one.

Format

- Briefly specify the fault and apologize for it or, in the case of a customer complaint, summarize the problem.
- Thank the person for writing or for calling or for bringing the problem to your attention.
- Appropriately, convey understanding of the other person's position.
- Tell what corrective action you're taking.
- Assure the person this won't happen again.
- In a business context, end the letter with a forward-looking comment about serving their future needs.

Models

Model 1

Dear Mr. and Mrs. Lamson, Please accept my apologies for missing your Thanksgiving brunch on November 23. I hope my last-minute change of plans	*First Apology*

did not bring inconvenience to you too much.	
As you know, I had planned on attending and was looking forward to it. However, my brother who lives in Boston, Georgia, had emergency surgery, and his wife asked me to be with her. Had that not happened, naturally I would have been with you.	*Explanation and Personal Comments*
Once again, I ask for your understanding in this matter and hope that my frantic, last-minute call to you was acceptable.	*Second Apology*
Sincerely,	
(Signature)	
Thomas Trundle	

Model 2

Dear Mr. Smith,	
I want to apologize for not having answered your very kind letter sooner, but I have been away on a trip and just returned today.	*First Apology*
The photographs you sent are beautiful. My family and I appreciate them very much. They are the best kind of remembrance, and we are very grateful.	*Personal Comments*
Again, please accept my apologies for the delay. And please give my best regards to your family.	*Second Apology*
Sincerely,	
Your student,	
Alfred Chace	

Model 3

Dear Dorothea,	
I feel dreadful about ruining your lovely luncheon yesterday by arguing with Celia about Will Ladislaw. You certainly did everything you could to save the situation, and I apologize most humbly for ignoring good taste, old friendship, and common sense in pursuing a "discussion" that was completely inappropriate.	*First Apology* *Understanding of the person's position*
I talked to Celia first thing this morning and attempted to mend my fences there, but I feel a great deal worse about what I did to you. The luncheon was delicious, and the first two hours were delightful. I hope you will someday be able to forgive me	*Tell what correct actions taken* *Second Apology*

for blighting the last half hour.

Your friend,
(writer's name)

Model 4

Dear Mr. Ravenal,

 As editor of the Cotton Blossom newsletter, I want to apologize for omitting your name in the last issue. Captain Hawks asked me how I could have possibly forgotten to include our hottest new actor! In proofreading the copy, my eyes failed to notice that your name wasn't where my brain expected it to be. I'm sorry. A correction will appear in the next issue.

First Apology

Explain the reason

Tell what correct actions taken

Regretfully,
(writer's name)

Model 5

September 15, 2022

Dear George,

 I'm writing to tell you that I've lost your copy of *Gone with the Wind*. I left it in the lounge, and someone must have picked it up. I'm really very sorry, and will try to replace it as soon as I can,

Regards,
(writer's name)

Useful Vocabulary and Expressions

Words

absent-mindedly	ill-advised	misleading	repay
accidental	imprudent	misprint	responsible
awkward	inaccurate	mistaken	restitution
blunder	inadequate	misunderstanding	short-sighted
careless	inconvenience	overlooked	tactless
compensate	insufficient	pardon	thoughtless
distressed	irresponsible	rectify	unaware
disturbed	misconception	regrettable	unintentional
embarrassed	misconstrued	reimburse	unsatisfactory
erroneous	misinterpreted	repair	unwarranted

Phrases

absolutely no excuse for	avoid this in the future
angry with myself	breach of good manners
appreciate your calling our attention	correct the situation
I am not excusing our/my errors, but	how can I apologize for
it was embarrassing to discover that	I am most upset about
it was most understanding of you to	reproach myself
I was distressed to hear/read/discover/learn that	prevent a recurrence
	sincerely regret/apologize
make amends/restitution	sorely regret
much to my regret	sorry for the inconvenience/confusion
my apologies for any inconvenience	to compensate for
owe you an apology for	under the mistaken impression that
please accept my/our apology/ apologies for	weighs on my mind
	we regret to inform our customers that

Sentences

I want you to know how sorry we are and to assure you that it won't happen again.

As you have pointed out, a mistake has been made on your July bill.

I am extremely embarrassed about my behavior last night.

I can only hope you will forgive this serious lapse of good taste on my part.

I hope this situation can be mended to everyone's satisfaction.

I'm sorry for telling everyone in the office your good news before you could tell them—I don't know what I was thinking.

I only realized later how insulting my remarks might have appeared.

I've taken steps to ensure that it won't happen again.

Please accept my apology for the oversight.

Please excuse my inattention/shortsightedness/thoughtlessness.

Thank you for advising us of this error/for bringing the matter to my attention.

Thank you for your patience and understanding. This will not happen again.

We apologize for the delay—it is unfortunately unavoidable.

Exercises

I. Read the following Apologies and match each part with a short description of what the writer is doing.

A.

Dear Hsiao-Wei,	In this part, the writer:
I apologize for not showing up at the meeting this afternoon. Although there is no excuse for such a thing, I will say that I was involved in an automobile accident on the way to work and what with filling out forms, notifying my insurance company, and arranging for a rental car, I completely forget about the meeting. Can we reschedule for this Thursday, same time? Thanks — and again, I'm sorry. Regards, (writer's name)	1._____ 2._____ 3._____

B.

Dear Merton Denscher,	In this part, the writer:
Thank you for your letter of March 19. I am sorry that the background research I submitted was unusable. A careful re-reading of your instructions showed me at once where I'd gone wrong. I do apologize. With your permission, I would like to resubmit the work — this time correctly. I believe I can get it to you by the end of next week since I am already familiar with the relevant sources for your topic. Sorry again, and please let me know at once if you prefer me not to go ahead. Sincerely, (writer's name)	1._____ 2._____ 3._____ 4._____

II. Write Apologies based on the information given.

1. Apology for the outspoken and insensitive remarks last night about religious convictions.

_____

2. Apology for upset suggestion.

_____

3. Apology for being unable to deliver the spring fabric samples by the date promised.

_____

Congratulations

Overview

Some of the most delightful words we receive are Congratulations. Because it is rarely obligatory and its contents are wholly positive, the congratulation note adds a glow to any personal or business relationship. And you don't have to wait for big news to send one. Small landmarks and successes have a sweetness all their own, and the recipient of your note will long remember your thoughtfulness.

Achievement of a milestone — a birthday or anniversary, birth of a new child, getting a new job, buying a house, winning an award, getting married— is an ideal reason to send someone a letter of congratulations. The reader will be pleased that you remembered the event and took the time to acknowledge it in writing.

Write soon after hearing the news. Congratulations are best sent timely. Even when you're close to the person to whom you're writing, make your congratulatory letter brief and somewhat formal, which may increase its impact.

Format

- Use the word "congratulations" early in your note.
- Mention the reason (graduation, promotion, honor, baby).
- Tell how happy, pleased, proud, or impressed you are and why.
- Tell how you learned about the good news. If you read it in the newspaper, enclose the clipping or photocopy of it.
- Relate an anecdote, shared memory, or reflection that has some bearing on the occasion.
- In closing, wish the person continued success; assure them of your affection, love, admiration, warmth, interest, delight, or continued business support.

Models

Model 1

Dear Tim,
 	
    Congratulations on your win in the Sci-Tech Innovation Competition held by Tsinghua University.
 	
    To be able to win at such a young age is quite an accomplishment. I understand that you not only won the Junior Division, but also came within points of the Senior Division winner.
 	
    Your mom is so proud of you. Congratulations once again!
 	
<div align="right">Sincerely,
Karen</div>
	First congratulation
	
	Personal comments (optional)
	
	Complimentary
	
	Second congratulation
	
	Closing

Model 2

Dear Parrish,
 	
    Wow! You've done it again. Congratulations!
 	
    I just read in NEPA Hotline that the direct mail package you wrote for Second Opinion just won a Gold Award for best promotion.
 	
    This is your third time, I believe. The client also gave you a wonderful plug in the article, noting that your DM packages for him have always been winners. That's an enviable track record few copywriters have ever achieved.
 	
    You must feel great, and I'm sure your clients are impressed, too. This should bring you a lot of new business.
 	
    Job well done, Parrish. I always learn a lot from you.
 	
<div align="right">Sincerely,
Ben Carter</div>
	First congratulation
	
	Tell how you learned about the good news
	
	Deep impression
	
	Relate an anecdote
	
	Reflection
	
	Your affection

Model 3

Dear William,
 	
    I've just heard from Katherine that you are finally a full-fledged chemical engineer — congratulations!
 	
    I've admired you as I've watched your struggles these past few years to acquire an education. Katherine and I said some rather flattering things about you and concluded that you're going to go far in this world.
 	
    My best wishes to you for a bright and happy future.
 	
<div align="right">Fondly,
Fishon Bringe</div>
	Tell how you learned about the good news
	
	Relate a shared memory
	Your happiness
	
	Wish a continued success

Model 4

Dear Mr. and Mrs. Miller,
 	
 Congratulations on the birth of your daughter Melissa. May you enjoy all the blessings of parenthood.
 With very best wishes!
 	
         Sincerely,
         David Jason
	Formal

Dear Martha and Tom, What wonderful news! I was delighted to hear about the baby and that you all are doing well! I want to congratulate both of you on the arrival of Melissa and wish you many years of happy parenting! love	*Informal*

Useful Vocabulary and Expressions

Words

accomplishment	exceptional	memorable feat	success
achievement	legendary	milestone	superb
admire	foresight occasion	momentous	superior
brilliant	genius	perseverance	superlative
celebration	gratifying	progress	talent
compliment	imaginative	prolific	thrilled
congratulate	impressed	recognize	tremendous tribute
contribution	incomparable	resourceful	triumph
creative	innovative	respected	unparalleled
dazzling	inspiring	satisfying	unrivaled
distinguished	invaluable	sensational	well-deserved
effort	inventive kudos		winner
esteem			

Phrases

accept my hearticst congratulations on	many congratulations and much happincss
achieved your goals	offer my warmest/sincerest/heartiest
all possible joy and happiness	congratulations
an impressive record/achievement	significant/valuable contribution
beyond all expectations	sincere wishes for continued success
couldn't let this happy occasion go by good/	spectacular achievement

great/sensational/joyful/thrilling news	take great pleasure in sending congratulations to you
high quality of your work	
in awe of all that you've done	were thrilled to hear about your important contribution
know that you're held in high esteem	
sharing in your happiness	you've done a superb job of

Sentences

- Baxter called this evening to tell us that the two of you are engaged to be married, and we wanted to tell you immediately how happy we are for you.
- Congratulations on opening your own office!
- Congratulations on the littlest Woodley—may she possess health, happiness, and love all her life.
- I am almost as delighted as you are with this recent turn of events.
- I hope we will enjoy many more years of doing business together.
- I just heard the news—congratulations!
- It was a splendid performance/great triumph/brilliant speech.
- I've just heard from XXX that two of your poems will be included in the next issue—congratulations!
- I very much admire your organizational skills/perseverance/many achievements/ingenuity/calm in the face of difficulties.
- My warmest congratulations on your graduation from Columbia!
- We've all benefited from your expertise and creativity.
- What terrific news!
- With best wishes for fair weather and smooth sailing in the years ahead.
- Your reputation had preceded you, and I see you intend to live up to it.
- You've topped everyone in the store in sales this past month—congratulations!

Exercises

I. Read the following Congratulations and match each part with a short description of what the writer is doing.

A.

	In this part, the writer:
Dear Mr. Donald, 　　Congratulations on the opening of your newest branch of the Revelation Motor Company. We have always appreciated doing business with you and expect to enjoy it even more now that your new office is only two blocks from us.	1._____ 2._____

Best wishes for happiness and success to all of you at Revelation.
 	
            Sincerely,
            (writer's name)
	3._____

B.

Dear Mr. Rochester,
 Congratulations on your election to the Thornfield School Board. I hope that after running such a vigorous and inspiring campaign you still have enough energy to carry out some of your sound and needed ideas.
 Be assured of our continued support, and do not hesitate to call on us if we can do anything to help.
 With best wishes.
 	
            Sincerely,
            (writer's name)
	In this part, the writer:
	1_____
	
	2_____
	
	3_____

II. Write Congratulations based on the information given.

1. Congratulations on receiving the Elite Student Award.

_____

_____

_____

2. Congratulations on the birth of little Laura.

_____

_____

_____

3. Congratulations on the election to the School Board.

_____

_____

_____

Application

Overview

An Application letter is a personal letter to a potential employer, mailed along with a copy of your résumé. The objective is to convince the reader that it would be in his best interest to admit or hire you or to at least invite you in for an interview.

Some organizations continue to rely on letters of application to evaluate an applicant's overall self-presentation and command of the written language.

The purpose of the application letter is to attract and hold the reader's attention long enough to get your letter placed in the list of the potential candidates who will receive an invitation to an interview. A letter of application is thus a sales letter in which you are both the seller and the product.

The most critical factor in getting an interview is how closely you match the prospective employer's needs. You already know what you have to offer, besides, you also need to know what the company needs from you. Call the company and ask questions; research the company at the library; speak to people who work there or who know the company. By presenting as clear a picture of yourself as you can in terms of what the company needs, you can make it easy for an employer to determine quickly whether you match the job. Avoid spelling or grammar errors, low-quality paper and poor spacing on the page.

Send an application letter to: camps, clubs and organizations, colleges and universities, internships, private elementary and secondary schools, volunteer organizations, etc.

Format

- Address your letter to a specific individual, after verifying the person's title and double-checking the spelling of the name.

- Open with an attention-getting sentence or paragraph.
- Tell why you are seeking this position, why you have chosen to apply for this particular company, and why you believe you are qualified.
- List the skills, education, and experience that are most relevant to the opening. Leave the rest for the interview.
- Request an interview.
- Provide an address, daytime phone number, fax number, and e-mail address.
- Close with a pleasant or forward-looking statement.

Models

Model 1

Dear Ms. Ronda,	*Address to a specific individual*
I would like to apply for the position of surgery scheduler for your ophthalmology practice.	
I received a two-year degree in office administration from Beckford Business College in 2019. Since then, I have worked full-time for Alasi Surgical Associates as a surgery scheduler.	*Tell the purpose of the letter* *Why qualified*
The work here has been more than satisfactory to me, but your clinic is half an hour closer to my home and I would like to shorten the commute time.	*Why seeking this position*
I can come for an interview any Saturday, or any weekday during the lunch hour, or after 17:30. If you leave an interview date and time on my home answering machine (555-1234), I will call to confirm.	*Ask for an interview by providing time and phone number*
Thank you.	
Best Regards, David Schimt	

Model 2

Dear Mr. Rudman,	
Enclosed is my résumé, which I am sending in response to your advertisement on the 51 Job website for a production engineer.	*Tell the purpose of this letter*
I am currently employed at Heavy Sheet Metal Company as one of three production engineers. I have complete responsibility	*List the skills*

Unit 8

for the sheet metal fabrication process from beginning to end. As you can see from my résumé, I have been a production engineer for the past five years.	
Please feel free to call me at my office during the day or at my home in the evening. Both numbers are listed on my résumé.	*Provide contact*
I will call you on Tuesday, January 17, to arrange a convenient time for us to meet if I have not heard from you before then.	*Request an interview*
I look forward to speaking with you. Sincerely, Maria Dong	*Close with forward-looking statement*

Model 3

Dear Margaret West,	
Libraries have been a second home to me for years, and I will be majoring in library science. In the meantime, I would like to apply for the summer job opening in your children's room.	*Application for an internship*
Although I lack of work experience (see résumé), I think I can offer you a deep and genuine interest in library science, a strong desire to excel at this kind of work, and library skills that come from many hundreds of library visits. As the oldest of the five children, I also have considerable experience and kindly bearing in dealing with young people.	*List the skills*
Thank you for your time and attention. Sincerely, Thruman Dougous	

Model 4

Registrar's Office State University Littleton, SD 55555 Dear Registrar:	
1 am a student of microbiology in Geneva, Switzerland. I would like to apply for entrance to your university. Would you please send me an application form and information on your	*Application letter to a university*

university?

Thank you.

Yours truly,
Renee Martin

Useful Vocabulary and Expressions

Words

abilities	education	opportunity	skills
apply	experience	professional	suitable
background	goals	qualified	
credentials	objectives	responsible	

Phrases

applying for the position of	may I have fifteen minutes of your time to discuss
arrange a meeting at your convenience	meet and exceed your criteria
experience that qualifies me for	similar to my most recent position
extensive experience with	skills that would be useful to
good candidate / match for the job	ten years' experience with
in response to your advertisement	well suited for
interested in pursuing a career with	

Sentences

- According to this morning's paper, you are seeking a ...
- After eight years as a senior analog engineer at ..., I am seeking a position in this area because of a family move.
- At the suggestion of ..., I am writing to request an interview for the project leader position in your fiber optic communications department.
- Because I believe you would find me to be an efficient, experienced, and dedicated legal administrative assistant, I am applying for the position at Wilson & Bean.
- Dr. Breuer has informed me that you are currently looking for a part-time veterinary technician.
- I am applying for the position of credit research analyst that you advertised in today's paper.
- I look forward to hearing from you.
- I understand from Dr. Hudson that you have an opening for a medical records supervisor.
- I understand that there is currently no opening in your office, but I would like you to keep my résumé on file and to consider me for any openings that occur.

- I will call you on Thursday to discuss setting up an interview.
- My eight years as a food microbiologist at XXX, Inc., make me eminently suitable for the responsibilities of the position you are currently advertising.
- Please consider me as an applicant for your advertised part-time position as clerical assistant in your business office.
- Thank you for considering my application.
- The skills and duties outlined in your advertisement in today's paper are almost a perfect match for the position I held until recently at XXX, Inc.

Exercises

I. Read the following Application letters and match each part with a short description of what the writer is doing.

A.

Dear Ms. Duchi, This letter is to request a job interview on the basis of referral. I am sending my résumé to you on the recommendation of Louis Divs of Splendid Paper Corporation. Louis told me that you were accepting applications for a product manager. I would be interested in talking with you to learn more about your company and the position. For the past four years, I have been at Greenwish Investment Products, Inc. Before that, I was at Laramy Products, Inc. The work I've done at these companies has given me a wide range of experience and an opportunity to develop skills that are essential to a product manager. I would welcome the opportunity to talk with you or to answer any questions about my background and career that you might have. You can reach me during the day at 180-1111-1111. Thank you for your consideration. Sincerely, (writer's name)	In this part, the writer: 1._____ 2._____ 3._____

B.

Dear Mr. Fitzpatrick,
 	
    For the past five years I have been successfully handling construction management in a very large general contracting business. I am now changing positions, and I feel that your organization might need my services.
 	
    I know both construction management and construction engineering. The following are some of my accomplishments:
 	
    • With Atlas Construction Co. during the past five years, I've had charge of the job site.
    • I have mastered the techniques of maintaining construction on schedule.
    • I have years of contract administration success.
    • I understand the value of cost control.
 	
    I am available at normal times. My résumé is enclosed.
 	
    For your current or future need, may I come in?
 	
                                     Very truly yours,
                                           Carl Messe
	In this part, the writer:
	
	1._____
	
	2._____
	
	3._____

II. Write Application letters based on the positions offered, and add source of information, related skills, reasons of application, contact information etc., which are necessary for an Application.

1. a security operation manager

_____
_____
_____

2. a receptionist for the new office who has fluency in seven language

_____
_____
_____

3. a branch manager

_____
_____
_____

Résumé

Overview

A résumé gives the prospective employers a written summary of your qualifications and work history. It convinces the reader that you're a good candidate for the position and that you should be invited for an interview. The résumé is a letter in which you are both the seller and the product.

When applying for a job, you might use one or two of the following: a résumé, a businesslike summary of your work history, education, career goals, letter of application, and a combination cover letter and brief.

Résumés are usually sent when applying for a job or internship, applying for membership in certain organizations, applying to universities/degree programs, inquiring about openings at a company, or responding to an employment ad.

Format

- Place your name, address, and daytime telephone number (and available e-mail address, fax number, and website address) at the top right or at the top center of your résumé (the top left position may get stapled or punched).
- State the position or kind of job you're seeking.
- Detail your work experience and job skills.

Tips on writing

- Before writing a résumé, assemble two kinds of information: facts about yourself and facts about your prospective employer and the position. You can emphasize certain skills and qualifications if you know that these are what the employer wants. When the prospective employers see a résumé that has obviously been written especially for them, they give it more attention. By presenting as clear a picture of yourself as you can in terms of the employer's needs, you can make it easy for them to determine quickly whether you match the job.

- Your résumé is only as long as it needs to be. Most authorities recommend no more than one or two pages, so your résumé must be tightly written and readable. Use simple, short sentences, keep paragraphs short, and leave plenty of white space and ample margins.
- Sample headings and divisions (you will generally have no more than five or six) that might be useful to you include:

Activities	Awards / Honors
Background Summary	Career Highlights
Career/Employment Objective	Education
Experience	Extracurricular Activities
Highlighted Qualifications	Office Skills
Leadership Skills	Overview of Qualifications
Negotiating Skills	Professional Affiliations
Organizational and Managerial Skills	Training
Professional Achievements/History	Supervisory Skills
Relevant Experience	Volunteer Work

- Use strong, active verbs like "I managed", "I developed", "I directed" instead of the weaker "I did this" or "I was responsible for that". Make all listings parallel in the form: "I supervised...I increased..." Not: "I was a supervisor...I have increased ...".
- Two tenses are used in a résumé: the present tense for categories like career goal and skills; the past tense for categories like work experience and professional accomplishments.
- You need not mention the reason for leaving a position. But the accepted reasons include: moving, returning to school, seeking a better position, unforeseen changes in your former job. Prepare a reason only for an interview.
- Don't use the same résumé for each job you apply for. Each résumé should be tailored to the particular company (no photocopies).
- Don't staple, glue, or seal your résumé. The pages should be loose and paperclipped together so that they are easier to handle. Mail your résumé and the cover letter in a big envelope so they arrive unfolded.
- Reference books of résumé writing: David F. Noble, *Gallery of Best Résumés: A Collection of Quality Résumés by Professional Résumé Writers*; Wendy S. Enelow,

Résumé Winners from the Pros.

Models

While an application letter persuades the reader to grant you an interview, the résumé presents the detailed facts of your employment history in an easy-to-scan format. The four basic types of résumé that this section provides are: executive, novice, chronological, and functional.

Model 1 EXECUTIVE RÉSUMÉS

For an experienced executive who has shinning working experience, the challenge is to compress a long job history into a one- or two-page résumé. Clear organization and concise writing are the keys to this type of résumé.

JOHN WILSON

5555 Parkside Avenue

New York, NY 02166

Telephone: (212) 555-5555

OBJECTIVE	Regional Director or Vice President, Group Sales — Insurance Industry
AREAS OF KNOWLEDGE	Group Life Insurance Accident and Health Insurance / Medical Care Insurance Sales / Sales Management / Sales Training Administration
EDUCATION	XXX University, Chicago, Illinois - B.S. Degree: Business Administration Minor: Marketing
EXPERIENCE	
2001 to Present	XXX Insurance Company, one of the very largest in the United States, offering complete coverage with all forms of life, health, hospital, and medical care insurance.
2010 to Present	Position: Group Account Executive (Regional Office) after promotion from Group Sales Supervisor. Report to Vice President. Responsibilities: — To personally manage and serve the extremely large group accounts annual premium range from $250,000 to many millions. — To maintain and build Company relations with Brokers and Insurance Consultants.

	– To represent the Company at the highest levels. Achievements: – Successfully handled complicated claim negotiations to the satisfaction of major policyholders and the Company. – Assisted in the underwriting and administration areas, involving the most important clients. – In 2010, qualified as Senior Account Executive
2001–2010	Position: Group Sales Supervisor after promotion from Sales Supervisor/Sales Trainee. Responsibilities: – Initially, to develop Group Life Sales to new accounts. – Since promotion to Chicago (2009), responsible for maintenance of large and vital Group accounts. – To train and assist Company agents in building Group Sales through prospect development. Achievements: – In 2007, was the 18th leading Company Sales Representative in the United States. – Sold over $221 million of new life insurance in 2008, climbing to No. 2 in the country. – Ranked first in the United States in 2009; $102 million of life insurance and $863 thousands of disability premium produced. – Built a reputation for achievement in personal sales along with an excellent conservation record and underwriting performance.
2001–2002	Position: Sales Supervisor/Sales Trainee, after promotion from Insurance Agent.
2000–2001	Position: Insurance Agent (Jasper, Indiana Office).
TRAVEL	Agreeable to any amount required to handle the position effectively.
LOCATE	Willing to relocate.
AVAILABILITY	30 days after final hiring commitment.
REFERENCES	Business and personal references immediately available upon request.

Model 2 **NOVICE RÉSUMÉS**

When you are a recent college graduate or otherwise lack extensive job experience, your challenge is to make what little you have seem like a lot. You have to elaborate and enhance your background and qualifications to make the résumé seem solid.

JUDE Wong

6372 Breaker Street, Cleveland, Ohio 12345

(216) 555-5555

STRENGTHS

- **Expertise in Finance**: Finance emphasis in both graduate and undergraduate studies. Broad base of knowledge and skills in a wide variety of finance applications. Strong desire to apply education to real-world situations.
- **Analytical Skills**: Analytical by nature. Solid problem-solving abilities. Research and investigation skills, including sourcing and fact-checking.
- **Personal Attributes**: Strong leadership skills. Decisive and goal-oriented. Effective in both individual and team competitive situations.
- **Communications**: Articulate, persuasive and quick thinking. Trilingual English/Mandarin/Indonesian.
- **Computers**: IBM PC. Experienced with DOS, Lotus 1-2-3, dBase, WordPerfect.

EDUCATION

M.S., New York University, New York City, New York, 1992-1993

B.A., XXX State University, XXX, Virginia, 1989-1992 (GPA: 3.9/4.0)

Coursework included

- **Finance**: Financial Management; Financial Reporting and Analysis; Financial Markets and Institutions; International Corporate Finance.
- **Banking**: Bank and Thrift Management; International Banking.
- **Investments**: Portfolio Management; Investments.
- **Management**: Business Development; Managerial Analysis and Communication; Business Policy and Strategy.

Accomplishments/Affiliations

- Treasurer, × × × Student Association. Managed revenues and funds. Developed and implemented programs to promote cooperation and friendship among MSA members, the university, and the community.
- Member, Asian Business Association.
- Member, Finance Student Association.
- Member, American Management Association.

Coursework included
- **Finance**: International Financial Management, Management of Financial Institutions.
- **Banking**: Monetary and Banking Theory.
- **Investments**: Security Analysis & Portfolio Management; Real Estate Investments.
- **Management**: Business & Its Environment; Business Policy; Management Information Systems.

Accomplishments/Affiliations

Vice President (× × × Student Association).

REFERENCES

Provided upon request.

Model 3 CHRONOLOGICAL RÉSUMÉS

The most common method to organize your résumé is in chronological order. You begin by listing your current job — company, title, job description — and then go back from there, listing all jobs held since you graduated from school.

The chronological method works well if you have been working steadily for a long period and have not been unemployed between jobs.

SAMUEL TAYLOR

55 North Drive Suburbia, Illinois 68301

Telephone: (312) 555-5555

Quality Control Manager, Electronics, Northwestern States

PROFESSIONAL EXPERIENCE

December 2015 to Present	Department Head, Quality Control, SSS Electronics Company. Responsible for customer acceptance of electronic components of airframe. Plan, schedule, and ensure timely completion of tasks of 200 employees. Report directly to Plant Manager.
June 2016 to December 2017	Supervisor, Quality Audit, SSS Electronics. Managed 10 employees. Responsible for adequate quality control procedures. Reported to Head of Quality Control Department.
May 2017 to June 2018	Chief, Quality Control Procedures, SSS Electronics. Edited and directed the work of five employees, providing all quality control procedures. Reported to Head of Quality Control Department.
August 2018 to May 2019	Technical Writer, published, and distributed test procedures for test stations and assembly operations.

PROFESSIONAL AFFILIATIONS

Member, American Society for Quality Control since 20—, President local chapter 20—, Member, Society of Technical Writers and Publishers since 20—, Senior member since

20—, President local chapter 20—, Secretary 20—.

EDUCATION

B.S. Industrial Management, XXX University, 20—.

Postgraduate studies include evening courses in Quality Control Concepts, Management Problems, Elements of Supervision, Engineering Statistics, and Labor Relations Problems.

PERSONAL

Will negotiate salary. Available within 30 days.

Model 4 FUNCTIONAL RÉSUMÉS

The functional résumé lists work experience by job title, job description, or work performed. It does not show chronology. Use a functional résumé when there are large gaps in your employment history.

SAMUEL TAYLOR

55 North Drive Suburbia, Illinois 68301

Telephone: (312) 555-5555

Quality Control Manager Electronics

EXPERIENCE

Quality Control Department Head, SSS Electronics Company. Manage 200 employees in a firm with a gross sale of $3.5 million. Familiar with all facets of quality control to electronics industry, having served in the present position for the past four years. Joined SSS in 2017 — as Chief Quality Control Procedures.

- Eliminated inspection bottlenecks by procedures change, saving $40,000 per year.
- Directed fabrication methods studies, reducing costs by 20 percent.
- Reduced inspection costs by 20 percent while reducing rejection rate saved $160,000.

PREVIOUS EXPERIENCE

Supervisor of Quality Audit, SSS Electronics, 20— to 20—.

Chief of Quality Control Procedures, SSS Electronics, 20— to 20—.

Technical Writer, VVV Electronics Corporation, 20— to 20—.

OTHER QUALIFICATIONS

Received B.S. in Industrial Management from XXX University 20—; graduated in upper third of class. Postgraduate studies include evening courses in Quality Control Concepts, Management Problems, Engineering Statistics, Labor Relations, and Supervision.

PERSONAL

Enjoy outdoors. Available within 30 days; do not contact employer.

Useful Vocabulary and Expressions

Words

accelerated	enlarged	infused	resourceful
accomplished	ensured	inspected	tactful
advocated	established	diversified	ambitious
accommodated	exceeded	enriched	conscientious
acquired	formulated	extended	assertive
boosted	implemented	elaborated	enthusiastic
challenged	doubled	equipped	intelligent
committed	educated	examined	qualified
completed	resolved	forged	self-confident
created	revitalized	initiated	trustworthy
designated	solved	translated	progressive
developed	steered	uncovered	responsible
leveraged	enthusiastic	unified	decisive
mastered	imaginative	upgraded	discreet
mended	intelligent	validated	efficient
multiplied	methodical		flexible
navigated	persistent		independent
pioneered	problem-solver		intuitive
predicted			motivated
prioritized			persuasive
promoted			productive
			reliable
			versatile

Phrases

I could contribute/have a strong aptitude for	analytical and critical thinking skills
experience that qualifies me for	extensive experience with
in response to your advertisement interested	good sense of/working knowledge of
in pursuing a career with	in this capacity
my five years as	qualities that would be useful in
sound understanding of	specialized in
supervisory abilities	take pride in my work
technical skills	well suited for
willing to travel	would enjoy attending/working

Sentences

- I am a skilled operator of the bridgeport mill and radial drill.
- I have three years' experience in product development.
- I met every deadline while working at XXX, some of them were under fairly difficult circumstances.
- In my last position I performed ... with minimum supervision.
- In my two years at XXX, I helped increase productivity by approximately 25% and decrease absenteeism by almost 20%.
- I successfully reduced stock levels while maintaining shipping and order schedules, resulting in lower overhead costs.
- I was responsible for all aspects of store management, including sales, personnel, inventory, profit and loss control, and overseeing the annual budget.

Exercises

I. Write a résumé for a computer science major college student who is about to hunting jobs in talent market. Write in the chronological style.

_____
_____
_____
_____

II. Write a résumé for an experienced product manager. Write in the functional style.

_____
_____
_____
_____

Recommendation

Overview

A letter of Recommendation tells a third party that the person is a responsible, functioning member of society. A letter of recommendation is more specific and focuses on the person's professional qualities and it is often written by someone who knows the applicant. If someone asks you in advance whether she/he can use you as a reference or have you write a referral letter, and you cannot in good conscience recommend her, say so. If you cannot write a good letter of recommendation, decline.

There are two specific types of letters of recommendation. In the first type, a friend or colleague asks you to write a "generic" letter of recommendation. It is not for a specific job or employer, but meant to be a general reference she can show to the interviewers if asked for such a letter.

In the second type, the employer asks the candidate for references, and the candidate gives your name. The employer asks you to recommend the person and tell the reason why.

When writing a Recommendation, try to be brief. One page, at most two, is sufficient to convey the general picture without repeating yourself. Be specific. Instead of saying someone is compassionate, tell how she/he missed a dinner party to help a troubled co-worker.

Format

The key to this letter is unbiased enthusiasm. Instead gush the praise, admit you're an unbiased promoter of the applicant. Let your enthusiasm shine through.

It will help the subject of the recommendation to have a signed, formal letter, which will probably appear more professional and credible to the recipient than an e-mail.

To write a convincing letter of recommendation, include:

1. A statement of wholehearted recommendation.

2. Exemplary adjectives.

3. Detailed examples of positive work habits.

4. A wish to retain the person in your own employ.

- Give the person's full name at the beginning of your reference or recommendation.
- State your connection with the person.
- Focus on the person's character for a general letter of reference.
- Emphasize job experience and skills and support your statements with facts or examples.
- Close with a summary statement reaffirming your recommendation of or confidence in the person.
- Offer to provide further information, if appropriate.

Models

Model 1

Dear Mr. Keyes, Because you're considering hiring Bonnie Denny as a customer service representative, let me do something I rarely do — recommend this former employee wholeheartedly.	*1. A statement of wholehearted recommendation*
I have seen customer service representatives come and go, and their quality varies. But Bonnie is the cream of the crop. Her skills are superb. In addition to being friendly, helpful, and articulate, she knew both our products and our buyers inside and out. By being an advocate for the customer, she is a champion of the company and firmly cements its relationship with the buyer.	*2. Exemplary adjectives* *3. Detailed examples of positive work habits*
After Bonnie moved east with her husband, who was relocated, a number of customers called me directly and complained that she was no longer available to talk to. If I had an office in your area, I would do anything I could to retain her as an employee and hire her away from you. But I don't, so she's yours to hire. Sincerely, (writer's name)	*4. A wish to retain the person in your own employ*

Model 2

If you have agreed to serve as a reference for a friend or acquaintance seeking a job, you may not want to write a separate letter for each position your friend is applying for. You can solve this problem by writing a blanket recommendation that the job seeker can show all the potential employers.

Prospective Employer,	
I am the Partner-In-Charge of ZZZ Industries, and I'm writing to recommend Tracy Gradon. I have known Tracy through her work experience with our firm during the past summer, when she served as an Audit Intern in our New York office.	*1. A statement of recommendation* *2. State the connection with the person*
Tracy became immediately involved in the annual audit of ZZZ Industries, conducting much of the historical accounting research required for the audit. In addition to gathering the financial information, Tracy was instrumental in the development of the final certification report. Tracy also participated in several other smaller audits, including her instrumental role in the quarterly audit of ABC Bank, where she developed several Excel macros to audit the inputs at the PC level. She later further developed these macros for the use in future audits, which we have integrated into our Auditors Toolkit.	*3. Exemplary adjectives* *4. Detailed examples of positive work habits*
Tracy has shown the kind of initiative that is necessary to be successful over the long term in the public accounting field. She has excellent forensic skills, yet remains focused on the overall needs of the client. I believe she will be a strong Auditor and has a bright future in the public accounting field. She is a conscientious worker and has an excellent work ethic. We would gladly have hired Tracy upon graduation if she were open to the New York City area.	*5. Reaffirm the recommendation*

I recommend Tracy to you without reservation. If you have any further questions with regard to her background or qualifications, please do not hesitate to call me.
                                      Sincerely,
                            Terry Thompson Partner-in-Charge
	6. Provide further information

Model 3

Here's another common situation: You agree to let someone use you as a reference, and when she does, the organization to which she is applying for a job contacts you for verification. To maximize the person's chance of getting the job, you want to write a letter of recommendation that is specific, positive, and concise.

Dear Mr. Villas,This is in response to your recent request for a letter of recommendation for Maria Rinnos who worked for me up until two years ago.	1. Connection with the person
Maria Rinnos worked under my direct supervision at Extension Technologies for a period of six years ending in October 2020. During that period, I had the great pleasure of seeing her blossom from a junior marketing trainee at the beginning, into a fully functioning Marketing.	2. Recommendation
She worked as the Program Co-Coordinator in her final two years with the company. That was the last position she held before moving on to a better career opportunity elsewhere.	
Ms. Rinnos is a hard-working self-starter who invariably understands exactly what a project is all about from the outset, and how to get it done quickly and effectively. During her two years in the Marketing Co-Coordinator position, I cannot remember an instance in which she missed a major deadline. She often brought projects in below budget, and a few were even completed ahead of schedule.	3. Detailed examples of positive work habits
Ms. Rinnos is a resourceful, creative, and solution-oriented person who was frequently able to come up with new and innovative approaches to her assigned projects. She functioned well as a team leader when required, and she also worked effectively as a team member under the direction of other team leaders.	4. Detailed examples of personality
On the interpersonal side, Ms. Rinnos has superior written and verbal communication skills. She gets along extremely well with the staffs under her supervision, as well as colleagues at the same level as her. She is highly respected, both as a person and a professional, by colleagues, employees, suppliers, and customers alike.	
In closing, as detailed above, based on my experience of working with her, I can unreservedly recommend Maria Rinnos to you for any intermediate or senior marketing position. If you would like further elaboration, feel free to call me at (555) 555-4293.Sincerely,Georgette Christenson Director, Marketing and Salesa	5. Reaffirm the recommendation and provide further information

Model 4

When someone asks you for a letter of recommendation, are you obliged to write it, even if you had trouble with the person in the past? This is a hard personal decision you have to make, but it would be dishonest to make a positive recommendation if it may hurt a potential employer. This course is better than agreeing to write the letter and then saying negative things.

Tell the person who requested the recommendation why you can't oblige, without name-calling or baiting. State the facts as you see them in a gentle but firm tone. Doing so, you have fulfilled your obligation to the request in an honorable way.

Dear Will,	
Thanks for your letter. It was good to hear from you again. I wish I could be of some help, but unfortunately, after giving it careful consideration, I feel I can't, in good conscience, write the letter of recommendation that you requested.	*1. A cordial greeting* *2. Your refusal to write the recommendation*
You are competent on the technical side of the business. But you and I had (and have) completely different perspectives on being a team player. I appreciate your desire to have time for creative thoughts and contemplation. But my feeling is, on a project team, you can't do so at the expense of meeting deadlines. As a result, other team members can't proceed to meet their milestones if you haven't met yours.	*3. A reason for your re-fusal. This can be a detailed account (while remaining professional and factual), or it can be a simple statement that says you do not share the same business philosophies*
While you were at this company, you worked for a number of other people with whom you may have had a better relationship. I'm sure that one of them would be glad to write you a positive letter of recommendation. Sincerely, (writer's name)	*4. A suggestion for finding a positive recommendation*

Useful Vocabulary and Expressions

Words

admirable	approve	conscientious	commendable
competent	congenial	dependable	considerate
cooperative	creative	effective	diligent
discreet	dynamic	ethical	efficient
endorse	energetic	hardworking	honest

experienced	first-rate	ingenious	initiative
imaginative	indispensable	invaluable	inventive
integrity	intelligent	outstanding	personable
praiseworthy	productive	professional	recommend
reliable	remarkable	resourceful	respect
responsible	self-motivated	sensible	successful
valuable	tactful	thoughtful	trustworthy

Phrases

broad experience/range of skills	acquits herself/himself well
creative problem-solver	discharged his/her duties satisfactorily
distinguished herself/himself by being a	do not hesitate to recommend
energetic and enthusiastic worker	have every confidence in
first-rate employee	highly developed technical skills
gives me real satisfaction to	in response to your request for
happy to write on behalf of	outstanding leadership abilities
have been impressed with	recommend with complete confidence
held positions of responsibility	satisfactory in every way
I wholeheartedly/highly recommend	set great store by sterling qualities
skilled in all phases of duties	take genuine pleasure in recommending
takes pride in his/her work	vouch for

Sentences

- Although the company policy prohibits me from writing you the recommendation you requested, I certainly wish you every success with your career.
- She has highly developed sales and marketing skills and has also proven herself invaluable in the recruiting, training, and supervising process of an effective sales team.
- He is one of our most knowledgeable people when it comes to custodial chemicals, equipments, and techniques.
- I am proud to recommend Ellen Huntly to you—I always find her work, character, and office manner most satisfactory.
- In response to your inquiry about Chris Nollin, it is only fair to say that ...
- I've known Richard Musgrove as a neighbor and employee for six years.
- I would prefer not to comment on Jean Emerson's employment with us.
- Thank you for the wonderful and apparently persuasive recommendation you wrote for me—I've been accepted by the Maxwell School of Political Science!
- To evaluate your suitability for the sales position you applied for, we need to speak to

at least four former employers or supervisors—please provide names, addresses, and daytime phone numbers of people we may contact.

• Working with you has meant a great deal to me and I'm wondering if I may give your name as a reference when I apply for my first "real" job.

Exercises

I. Read the following Recommendation letters and match each part with a short description of what the writer is doing.

A.

Dear Mr. Collins, I have known Steve Monk for four years, first as a student in my earth sciences and biology classes and later as Steve's adviser for an independent study in biology. I am currently helping him with an extracurricular research project. Mr. Monk is one of the brightest, most research-oriented students I have encountered in eighteen years of teaching. His SAT and achievement test scores only begin to tell the story. He has a wonderful understanding of the principles of scientific inquiry, a passion for exactitude, and a bottomless curiosity. I am interested in Steve's situation and will be happy to provide any further information. Sincerely, (writer's name)	In this part, the writer: 1._____ 2._____ 3._____

B.

Dear Sir or Madam, At the request of Mr. Xizhen Chen, my former student in the Department of Computer Science, Beijing University of Sciences, I am glad to write this letter furnishing my evaluation of his academic aptitude for your reference. Mr. Chen is interested in your graduate program in Computer Science. I came to know him in September 2017 when Mr. Chen enrolled in my class on FORTRAN IV Programming, a three semesters' course. In the class he was one of the most outstanding students. At the semester final exam he earned a high score of 81, which should be "A" according to our grading system. I also found	In this part, the writer: 1._____ 2._____ 3._____

him good at other studies. After the class, he had personal talks with me several times. He indicated a great interest in computer hardware. In my opinion, Mr. Chen has a potential in Computer Science, which can be further developed. In view of his previous achievements in this College, I am firmly convinced that Mr. Chen will make a successful graduate student. Your favorable consideration of his admission will be highly appreciated.

Sincerely,
(writer's name)

II. Write Recommendation letters based on the information given.

1. Name: Wang Yong

   Identity: favorite student

   Issue: for admission into a PhD program

   Character: Won Gifted Youths award at the age of 14

   　　　　　Outstanding self-study capability

   　　　　　High score in exam

   　　　　　Noticeable progress in English proficiency in short time

   　　　　　Intelligent, ambitious, persistent

   _____

   _____

   _____

2. Name: Mr. Deng

   Identity: former student graduated 5 years ago

   Issue: transfer to the School of Business of your University in the next semester

   Character: intelligent and diligent

   　　　　　excellent extracurricular activities experience

   　　　　　honest, reliable, responsible and mature

   _____

   _____

   _____

   _____

Business Correspondence

Communication is a critical part in any sphere of a human activity. But first of all, it is important to business. Businesses want and need people with good communication skills. Good writing is "you-centered", not "I-centered". Rather than thinking about demonstrating what you know, you should think about what your potential reader needs to know or can gain from reading your writing.

1. Selecting the right words. Use of active voice, nonsexist words, and neutral expressions is the guide for business writing. Right words are the words that communicate best—that have correct and clear meanings in the reader's mind. Selecting the right words depends on your ability to use the language, knowledge of the reader, and your good judgement.

2. Writing in a brief way. Most business writers today attempt to fit their entire letter on one side of a single sheet of company letterhead, which asked for brevity.

3. Conducting clear writing. Clear writing involves using a simpler sentence structure to reach people with lower communication skills. As you move along, you should view these basics as work tools in communication.

4. Using positive language in order to get the results you want. As you can see as follows, the column on the right turns the negative words into positive words to obtain a positive reader response.

Negative	Positive
We are unable to promote you to supervisor because you do not have the skills and experience required for this position.	We will be able to promote you to supervisor when you meet the requirements of this position.
We will not start repairing your test equipment until we receive a deposit.	We will begin repairing your test equipment once we receive a deposit.
If you fail to provide the deadline, the project will fail.	By providing the specifications, the project will be on time.
The corporation will not pay unless employees also contribute.	The corporation will pay only if employees contribute.

You neglected to send us your passport copy and therefore we cannot process your request.	We will be able to process your request as soon as we receive a copy of your passport.
I hope that you will not be disappointed with the quality of our report.	I am sure that you will be delighted with the quality of our report.
We cannot send your order from our store until June 1, 2022.	Your order will be sent to you on June 1, 2022.
You failed to include your company number, so we cannot process your application.	We will be glad to process your application as soon as we receive your company number.
This problem would not have happened if you had connected the wires properly in the first place.	This problem may be resolved by connecting the wires as shown in the handbook.

Make sure that the words and expressions you choose to get the results are not those you have much stress on "not", "no" or "never".

In this section, model letters for a wide range of business situations will be presented, from sending a follow-up letter to a contact, to requesting a favor from someone. Most of these models can be used interchangeably as either a letter, a fax, or an e-mail. A more practical use of these letters is to guide you in how to say things that you have often had difficulty saying in the past—for example, requesting a favor, giving instructions, saying yes, or saying no. Perhaps in the letters here you will find just the right phrase for those difficult moments, and save time, money, and frustration as a result.

Requests and Inquiries

Overview

Letters of request (when you want to ask for something) and letters of inquiry (when you want to know something) are critical in maintaining the flow of ideas and resources among individuals and organizations. Because they are often the first contact between businesses and potential customers, between those seeking something and the employers, publishers, and vendors they are seeking it from, these letters must be good ambassadors.

Most commonplace requests (to change a life insurance beneficiary, to claim insurance benefits, to apply for a VA loan, to purchase a home, for federal employment) are initiated by a phone call and completed with the appropriate forms. Only in the case of problems are letters required.

There are many other occasions when you need to ask for information, for a favor (e.g., asking a colleague to refer you to someone you want to meet), for a deadline change, or for permission to reprint something — it's just part of doing business. There are some tips for writing a Request/Inquiry:

- Be brief, avoiding unnecessary explanations or asking the same question in two different ways.
- Be precise about the information you want. The more information you give, the more helpful is the information you receive.
- Not to end a letter of request with "thank you" or "thanking you in advance". Instead, you can end with "I appreciate your time and attention" or "I look forward to hearing from you".
- Make it easy for someone to respond to you: enclose a survey or questionnaire; provide a postage-paid postcard printed with a message and fill-in blanks; leave space

under each question on your letter so the person can jot down replies and return it in the accompanying self-addressed stamped envelope(SASE).

Format

If you're a business owner, you are likely to have a number of reasons to write several business request letters, such as requests for more information or requests for payments. However, once you create a well-written, professional template for these kinds of letter, then you can easily modify it in order to accommodate any of your future needs and therefore save a great deal of time. The following are the guidelines for writing a request:

- State clearly and briefly what you're requesting.
- Give details to help the person send you exactly what you want (reference numbers, dates, descriptions, titles, etc).
- If appropriate, briefly explain the use you intend to make of the material.
- State the specific action or response you want from your reader.
- Explain why your reader might want to respond to your request.
- If appropriate, offer to cover the costs of photocopying, postage, or fees.
- Specify the date by which you need a response.
- At the end, if your letter is a long one, restate your request.
- Express your thanks or appreciation for the other person's time and attention.
- Enclose a self-addressed stamped envelope (SASE), if appropriate.
- Otherwise, tell where to send the information or where to telephone, fax, or e-mail the response.

Models

Model 1

Dear Mr. Rytik,
 	
    We are trying to locate information on a breed of cat called the Suomi shorthair and understand that you are the leading expert on cats in Finland.
 	
    We have a client who is interested in buying a Suomi short-hair. She had seen one once at the New York Feline Show but has been unable to locate one since. She came to our ship and requested that we help her. Since the breed originated in Finland, we thought you might be able to give us some more information. We are most interested in the names of breeders that may have kittens for sale.
	Inquiry Compliments
	
	Explanation

We will call you within the next month to follow up on this inquiry. Thank you for all your trouble. We look forward to talking to you. Sincerely, (Signature) Kathleen "Cat" Pence	*Contact information* *Thank You*

Model 2

Dear Sir/Madam, 　　We are a smartphone company, and we are going to hold an annual sales conference. We saw you on the Internet ads.	*Reasons*
We would like to know more about the facilities and information of Sun Hotel. Could you tell us if it is convenient for you to offer a conference hall for 50 people with excellent acoustics to demonstrate our new products from July 1st to July 3rd?	*Requests*
It would also be much helpful if audio and visual equipments such as OHP (Overhead Projector), flipchart and video are available for us. And we would also like to be told whether there are enough rooms, preferably single room and whether three meals are served for 50 people every day during that time. We also care about the prices. We shall be obliged if you will offer us some information in detail.	*Details of requests*
We look forward to hearing from you by return before June 15, if possible. SASE is attached. Thank you! Yours faithfully, Roger Guan Manager	*Specify the time* *SASE enclosure*

Model 3

TO: Emmerick Demolition and Salvage 　　In September 2022 you submitted a bid to Brooker Real Estate to remove two structures, one at 1898 Stratfield and the other at 1921 Cabell. Since that bid, two additional properties have been purchased by Brooker Real Estate that will require demolition this summer.	*Reasons* *What needed to be done*
I invite you to submit a rebid to include the two additional sites plus tank removal at another site (please see attachment for	*More requests*

the description and addresses of sites). Contact me if you submit a bid as I would like to schedule a meeting to discuss this project further and to answer your questions. Sincerely, Thomas Stevenson Manager	

Model 4

Dear Mr Warden,	
Would you please supply information and recommendations on the type of refrigerator we might install in two-bedroom apartments?	*Requests*
Ninety-six refrigerators will be needed for our new apartment building, which is scheduled for completion within four months. Four other buildings now under construction in the same complex will need new appliances later.	*Explanation*
Because we are considering your company as one of the suppliers, please answer the following questions: 1. What size is appropriate for two-bedroom apartments? 2. Do you recommend putting self-defrosting refrigerator in rental units? 3. Do you provide after-sales service for the refrigerators you sell? If so, how quickly can you repair them in case of breakdown? 4. What models of apartment-sized refrigerators do you carry? And what are their prices?	*Ask for details*
The refrigerators must be ordered within a month, so we would appreciate receiving your reply by November 25. Sincerely, Harry Williams	*Specify the time*

Model 5

Dear Ms Allison,	
Thanks for your letter dated Nov. 8, 2011, expressing your interest in our Auto parts.	*Locate the source*
Enclosed please find our latest catalogue, price list and a booklet regarding our new line of parts for your consideration. You will get a special discount of 5% if you place an order over 5,000 sets.	*Specify the information provided*

Since we are a well-experienced and specialized maker and exporter in this line in China, we will be able to offer you the top-quality products at low prices. Due to the increasing demand for the parts in the market, we will be forced to raise our price in the near future. We suggest you order from us before March 2012.	*Explain the validity of price*

We hope you will give us the chance to provide you with our best quality products.
 	
             Sincerely yours,
              Tony Bruces
	Close with good will

Model 6

Dear Danielle,	
Thanks for the big notebook and the customer service book. Both are at your usual high level of excellence.	*Thanks for the offer*
Unfortunately, the answer to your question is no. I'm unable to take on any additional projects right now because I'm already too busy.	*Explain the reason of refusal with regret*
If you need further help down the line, be sure to let me know. Hopefully, my schedule will open up and allow me take on an interesting work like this at a later date.	*Offer alternative action*

I wish you luck with the project.
 	
               Best regards,
               Tony Bruces
	Close with a pleasant wish

Useful Vocabulary and Expressions

Words

appeal	assistance	brochures	expedite
favor	furnish	generous	grant
grateful	immediately	information	inquiry
instructions	products	prompt	problem
query	require	questionnaire	quickly
refer	solicit	urgent	reconsider

Phrases

additional information/time	apply/ask for
anticipate a favorable response	count on/upon
appreciate your cooperation/your help	have the goodness to
direct me to the appropriate agency	I'd appreciate receiving/obtaining
	institute inquiries

if you can find time in your busy schedule to	I would be grateful/most grateful if/for
I would appreciate your assessment of	offer some assistance
look forward to hearing from you	on account of/behalf of
please call me to discuss	please let me have your estimate by
please provide us with/send details about	please reply by
reply by return e-mail to	thank you for your efforts in/to

Sentences

- Can you tell me which government agency might be able to give me the background information on ...?
- Enclosed is a self-addressed stamped envelope/an International Reply Coupon for your reply.
- I am preparing a report for ... — can you provide these by March 15?
- I'm wondering if you have the time to give us a little guidance.
- I would be interested in seeing some of the material that went into the preparation of your most recent occupational titles handbook.
- May I use your name as a reference when applying for a cashier position ...?
- Please forward this letter to the appropriate person.
- Please send me any literature you have on ...
- We do not understand the footnote (b) of Exhibit H — could you please explain it?
- Will you please send me a copy of your current foam and sponge rubber products catalog along with the information on bulk order discounts?

Exercises

I. Write an Inquiry letter based on the following information given.

Your work at Hardstone involves investigating applicants for employment. This morning the Personnel Department sends you information about Mr. Brown, who is a likely candidate for the vacant position of office manager. After talking with Mr. Brown, you feel that he is bright and personable. But to make the final decision, you feel that you must follow the usual practice of asking references for the evaluation of the candidate. In this case, the best possibility is Ms. June Bayer, the former immediate supervisor of Mr. Brown for 2 years.

Your task is to write Ms. Bayer a letter to get the information such as Mr. Brown's leadership, stamina and drive, moral reliability, etc.

II. Make a response to the following request.

Dear sir,

We know your firm from the ads in the magazine. We are interested in your washing machines, particularly Model 3256, for use in factory. Would you please send us a copy of your illustrated catalogue and the latest price list?

We look forward to hearing from you.

                       Yours sincerely,

                       (writer's name)

_____

_____

_____

III. Write an Inquiry letter and a reply letter based on the following condition.

1. 我方是哥本哈根东部的一家纺织品经销商，有着多年从业经验。从我驻外使馆商务参赞处了解到，对方是全棉床罩和枕套的主要出口商，写信给对方以建立业务关系，并索要对方的商品目录和价目单。

Key points

1. 从事纺织品进口
2. 求购高质量的全棉床罩和枕套
3. 进行询盘
4. 简单介绍市场的需求
5. 表达订单的可能性

_____

_____

_____

2. 出口商在收到询盘信后，给予答复。随信寄了几本带有插图的商品目录和一份价目单。另外，为了证明产品的质量及工艺，单独邮寄了一些样品。信中还提出对成批购买给予3%的优惠，凭不可撤消即期信用证付款。

Key points

1. 给予答复
2. 寄出目录、价目单和样品
3. 对付款方式和折扣优惠进行回答

_____

_____

Orders

Overview

An Order Letter is usually written to assign orders or place order of goods. The letter is written in a very precise and specific manner. This letter comes into action only when a detailed study of the desired product has been done in the market and based on promised service, quality and price of the product, a decision for a purchase has been made.

An Order Letter should be drafted very carefully and have details such as product specifications, quantities, price agreed upon, delivery date, late delivery clauses, etc.

Confirmation of orders basically summarizes the verbal agreement that was previously made between the two parties. People in the business world, usually make use of such a letter as a formal document in order to maintain it as a record and acknowledge a particular task. The cancellation letter is used for a business correspondence in order to convey the act of cancelling. However, there can be many reasons to write a cancellation letter but whatever the reason may be, it is important to make use of polite tone.

When ordering, give: description of the desired item, quantity, size, color, personalization/monogram, and price. Include your name, address, zip code, daytime phone number, e-mail address, and method of payment.

Indicate the date by which items must be delivered. You can thus generally cancel the order without forfeit if you don't receive it in time; the letter serves as an informal contract.

To respond to orders received, use an all-purpose form for problems. Begin with "Thank you for your order. We are unable to ship your merchandise at once because..." and list the possible problems so that one or more can be circled, underlined, or checked off. For example: "Payment has not been received." "We no longer fill C.O.D. orders." "Please send a check or money order." "We cannot ship to a post office box." "We no longer carry that item." "May we send a substitution of equal value and similar style?" "Please indicate the size (quantity, style, color)." "We must receive shipping and handling charges before processing your order."

Format

Accuracy is essential in the placing of an order—an error in quoting a catalogue number, or a mistyped figure in the quantity column can cause trouble which may be impossible to put right later.

Clarity is also essential. The buyer must make clear to the seller exactly what he wants: exact description of the goods, method of transport, packing, delivery and insurance, or possible method of payment. When ordering goods, a customer will generally include the following in his letter:

A reference to a visit by the supplier's representative, or to an ad, or catalogue, or to a sample, or to previous correspondence. This applies particularly to a first order. In subsequent orders the buyer may begin his letter with:

- Details of goods requirements: quantity, quality, catalogue number, packing, etc.
- Conditions and qualifications.
- Alternatives which are acceptable if the goods ordered are not available.
- A closing sentence, encouraging the supplier to execute the order promptly and with care.

Models

Model 1

Purchasing Department, 　　I would like to order the following books in cloth or hardback: 　　1) Chatting Times by Ralph Wright, United Press, 1980, one copy, 　　2) Music for Milsons by Nellie Blum, Great Books Co., 1956, three copies,	*Details of goods requirements*
3) General Geology by Harwood and Brown, Scott Book Co., 1984, one copy,	
Would you please send me the list prices and shipping costs as soon as possible? 　　Thank you. 　　　　　　　　　　　　　　　　　　　　Sue Ellen Appleton 　　Mailing address:	*Payment*

87 Broad Street North Dry Gulch, NM 55566	

Model 2

Dear Mr. Pereira, 　　With reference to our meeting on 14th December, we would like to inform you that the order of 20,000 horn covers has been approved. You have to deliver the same in 30 days. Please find the details on color and number of pieces below:	*Locate the occasion*
Item　　　　　Color　　Piece　　　　　　Amount 　Horn Covers　Grey　　$250 per piece　　10,000 　Horn Covers　Beige　　$250 per piece　　10,000	*Details of requirements*
I am enclosing a cheque of $ 20,000 as advance payment. The rest payment will be done after delivery.	*Payment*
Please feel free to contact me if you need any sort of clarification. And please dispatch the goods latest by 14th January.	*Date of execution*
We hope to have a long-term business association with you. 　　　　　　　　　　　　　　　　　　　　　　　Yours truly, 　　　　　　　　　　　　　　　　　　　　　　　(writer's name)	*Good wish*

Model 3

Dear Sir or Madam, 　　Thank you for your previous letters and having sent us samples of canned mushroom. We find both quality and prices satisfactory and are pleased to place an order for the following goods on the understanding that they will be supplied from stock at the prices stated:	*Reasons of purchase*
Quantity　　Article No.　　Prices 　12M　　　　Ts0801　　　　USD1800 per M/T 　8 M　　　　Ts0802　　　　USD1800 per M/T 　FOB Yantai.	*Details of requirement*
Our usual terms of payment are by D/P at sight and we hope that they will be acceptable to you.	*Payment*
Please send us your confirmation of sales in duplicate and see to it that the goods are strictly in accordance with the samples.	*Confirmation needed*
If this first order is successfully executed, we shall place further and larger orders with you in the near future. 　　　　　　　　　　　　　　　　　　　　　　Yours sincerely, 　　　　　　　　　　　　　　　　　　　　　　(writer's name)	*Close with pleasant wish*

Model 4

Dear Sir or Madam,	
We acknowledge with thanks to your kind order of Sept. 2 for stationeries. It has our immediate and careful attention. We are sending you here with our Sales Confirmation No. 1384 in duplicate. Please sign and return one copy to us for filling.	*Confirmation of order with file No.*
Paying our best attention to the execution of this order, we have carefully packaged the articles. You may rest assured that we shall effect transportation through EMS upon reception of the credit. It is understood that the letter of credit in our favor shall be established immediately.	*Assurance of execution of order*
Thank you for your patronage. We sincerely hope that this will lead to an enduring connection with you.	*Close with pleasant wish*
Best regards, (writer's name)	

Model 5

Dear Dr. Sturmthal,	
Thank you for your purchase order # H459991, which we received on June 3, for the TEM-500 Transmission Electron Microscope. Your order has been sent to our Administration Department and your Purchasing Department will be advised directly as to the confirmation of terms and shipping dates.	*Confirmation of order with file No.*
Teresa Desterro, Manager of the Sales Department, located in our Gillespie office, will advise you of the confirmed delivery dates and can provide you with answers to questions on order processing or shipment expediting.	*Assurance of execution of order*
Alec Loding, National Service Manager, also located in our Gillespie Office, will send you complete information on the installation requirements of your new TEM-500. Both Ms. Desterro and Mr. Loding can be reached directly by calling 212/555-1212.	*Details of execution of order*
We appreciate your order and the confidence you have shown in our company and in our instruments. We look forward to hearing from you either now or in the future if there is any way in which we may be of assistance to you.	*Close with pleasant wish*
Sincerely yours, (writer's name)	

Model 6

Dear Customer, As you requested [in our meeting of ...], we are preparing to make the following changes to [name of project]:[summarize changes here, preferably in a numerical list]	*Changes*
Although we have attempted to minimize the impact of these changes wherever possible [through such measures as ...], they will nonetheless increase the total of our proposal of [date] [which I have revised and attached] by $10000.	*Reasons for the changes*
The good news is that we do not anticipate these changes will affect the schedule. We will continue to try to reduce the impact of these changes as the project goes forward.	*Willingness to continue the business*
Please indicate your approval and return this letter to me as quickly as possible so we can avoid any delays that might further affect the price or scheduling. It would not be appropriate to continue work without your agreement.	*Ask for feedback*
If you wish to discuss the impact of these changes with me, please call XXXXXX.	*Contact*
Thanks again for the privilege of working with your company. We're looking forward to producing a world-class [type of project] for you. <div align="right">Sincerely, (writer's name)</div>	*Thanks*

Useful Vocabulary and Expressions

Words

billed	cancel	change	charge
confirm	deposit	expedite	freight
goods items	handling	immediately	invoice
receipt	merchandise	overnight stock	overpayment
urgent	warehouse		underpayment

Phrases

confirm your order	hereby confirm
enclosed is my check for	must cancel my order of
I would like to order next-day delivery	please advise us/let us know
please bill to retail/wholesale price	prompt attention
ship C.O.D.	return receipt
being shipped to	requested shipping and handling charges

Sentences

- Along with your order I'm enclosing our spring catalog as I think you'll want to know about our new lower prices.
- If you cannot have the storage cabinets here by October 3, please cancel the order and advise us at once.
- Please bill this order to my account # JO4889 at the usual terms.
- Please cancel my order for the Heather stone china (copy of order enclosed)—the three-month delay is unacceptable.
- Please charge this order to my Carlyle First Bank Credit Card # 333-08-4891, expiration date 11/04 (signature below).
- Please check on the status of my order # 90-4657 dated March 1.
- Please confirm receipt of this order by fax or telephone.
- We are pleased to inform you that both your orders were shipped this morning.
- Your order # KR45G is being processed and should be shipped by August 1.

Exercises

I. Choose the appropriate word or words.

1. We are arranging for the punctual (shipment, shipping) of the (ordered, order) goods.

2. Our offer is (firm, work) subject to your reply (for, in, within) one week.

3. Any delay (in, about) shipment will cause us inconvenience.

4. Enclosed is our order (for, on) 300 sets of Transistor Radio.

5. Your (term, terms) are satisfactory and we are pleased to (enclose, place) an order (with, to) you.

6. If you cannot (send, give) the goods as per (requirements, specifications), please send us the alternates.

7. If you do not have Model 105 (from, in) stocks, please (remove, cancel) this order.

8. We hope you will (agree, accept, receive, admit) our terms and make (preparation, arrangements) for an early delivery.

9. We (admit, acknowledge) with thanks your order of June 1.

II. Fill in the blanks with the phrases in the box.

| together with | place regular orders | in case | in accordance with |
| in duplicate | in one's favor | shipment | in due course |

1. _____ the faxes exchanged between us; we are pleased to confirm having purchased from you 10,000 dozen men's shirts of "Haida" Brand.

2. If the quality of your machine is satisfactory and your prices are suitable, we expect to _____ for fairly large numbers.

3. Enclosed please find our Purchase Confirmation NO.8848 _____.

4. Please let us know _____ you are interested in any of the items.

5. We will open an L/C _____ in time.

6. Upon receipt of your L/C, we will effect _____ of your order without delay.

7. We have received your letter of Feb.25 _____ a draft contract showing the terms and conditions of your sale.

III. Translate the following sentences into English.

1. 我公司对贵公司各种型号的自行车感兴趣，决定试订一批。

2. 我方客户急需这些货物，望早日发货装运为盼。

3. 有关的信用证已由中国银行上海分行开立。在收到信用证后，请安排装船，并以传真告知船名及起航日期。

4. 接受订单后三周内交货，货款以不可撤销的信用证、凭即期汇票支付，海险由我方承保。

5. 贵方9月20日第WG721/BP号订单已收阅，谢谢。

6. 很抱歉，由于大量承约，我们暂不能接受你方一千台电脑的订单。

IV. Read the below order letter carefully and then write a confirmation letter to the buyer.

Dear Sirs,

We have received with thanks your letter of February 21 and all samples. We have now examined your samples and are satisfied with both quantity and prices. Please accept our order for the following items:

1200 doz. silk handkerchiefs at $2.00 each, $2400

2000 pair tan pig skin leather shoes, size 6 at $4.00 each, $8000

3000 doz. assorted orlon socks at $1.50 each, $4500

TOTAL $14,900

Delivery: By the end of March, 2001

Payment: Draft at sight under irrevocable L/C

Invoice: Commercial Invoices in triplicate

The order No. 16 must be stated on all invoices and correspondence. Final shipping instructions will be enclosed later. We request you to acknowledge acceptance of our order, and to confirm the condition stated above.

Faithfully yours,

Peter Anderson

Complaints

Overview

If you're writing a letter of complaint, you're not alone. Ideally, it should not be necessary to complain, since in business everything should be done so carefully—details of offers and orders checked, packing supervised, quality control carried out expertly—that no mistakes are made and nothing is damaged. Unfortunately, as in other walks of life, things do not work out as well as that. Errors occur and goods are mishandled; accidents happen, usually because of haste and lack of supervision.

In general, a letter of complaint is more effective than a phone call. First, you've put something tangible on someone's desk—eventually it must be dealt with. Second, you can be more tactful in a letter. Third, the details are conveyed in an accessible form. Fourth, you have a record of your complaint.

Complaints may be of several kinds, and may arise from the delivery of wrong goods, damaged goods, or too many or too few goods. Even if the right articles are delivered in the right quantities, they may arrive later than expected, thus causing severe difficulty to the buyer and, possibly, to his customers. Then the quality of the goods may be unsatisfactory: perhaps they are not according to the sample or description the basis of which they were ordered, or they may simply be second-rate products.

If a customer is dissatisfied with the execution of his/her order, he/she will complain. In doing so, he/she should refer clearly to the articles in question, by referring to his/her own order number or to that of his/her supplier's invoice, or both. He/she should then specify the nature of his/her complaint, and finally state what action he/she wants his/her supplier to take.

As a businessperson, not only get complaints from customers, you may often find yourself in a position to be making a complaint. The following part of this unit will help you find the way you need when things aren't going right and you want to tell someone about it.

Format

- State the problem: what it is, when you notice it, how it inconveniences you.
- Provide factual details.
- Include relevant documentation: sales slips, receipts, warranties or guarantees, previous correspondence, pictures of damaged item, repair or service orders, canceled checks, contracts, paid invoices.
- Tell why it's important to resolve your problem.
- State clearly what you expect from the person or company: refund, replacement, exchange, repair. Request a reasonable solution.
- Suggest a deadline for the action.
- Give your name, address, and home and work telephone numbers.

Models

Model 1

Dear Richard, I am writing because I feel that the communication between us is deteriorating and will soon affect my ability to continue doing business with your firm. I have found that in the past month I cannot discuss our company sales policies without feeling very defensive, faced with your immediate negative responses.	*1. Statement of your complaint*
The example that comes quickest to my mind occurred last Friday. If you remember, I simply wanted to ask if it was possible to transfer your discount credit to next month's order but ended up arguing the value of the discount policy in general.	*2. Specific details of the problem*
I value our relationship very much and I think you have a terrific service to offer. But our ability to do business suffers when our communication breaks down and we don't understand each other. If you have complaints about our overall business arrangement, please let me know so that we can get the problem out in the open. Otherwise, I need you to listen before you start arguing when I call with a question. Let's try this one again: "Is it possible to transfer your discount credit to next month's order?"	*3. An acknowledgment of the value of your relationship* *4. A course of action you would like the recipient to take*

I look forward to continuing our business relationship in a positive and cordial manner.
 	
                                                  Sincerely,
                                                  (writer's name)
	5. A cordial and upbeat ending

Model 2

Dear Sheldon,	1. *The name*
This letter will confirm our correspondence regarding the deadline for the Handbook of Telecommunications Acronyms and Standards. As I noted in our conversation, we expect to receive the complete manuscript, including revisions and any new text, in hard copy and on a USB drive by December 28. This deadline is an extension of the December 10 deadline that was set with Betsy Shephard on November 19.	*of the project you're writing about* 2. *The dates involved* 3. *The reason*
We cannot extend the deadlines any further nor can we delay this publication any longer. Therefore, the above submission deadlines need to be met so we can meet our publication schedule.	*the delay is not acceptable* 4. *The current*
I look forward to receiving your manuscript and USB drive on December 28. If you have any questions, please contact me at 123-456-7890. Sincerely, (writer's name)	*deadline* 5. *An offer to answer any questions*

Model 3

To: Jim Burke, Group Product Marketing Director From: Alex Freeman Re: Ad agency services purchasing procedure Dear Jim,	1. *The topic of your complaint*
I just received the Approved Agency list. According to the memo, we may purchase creative and production services only from a list of six approved agencies.	2. *The exact reasons for your complaint*
I think this is counterproductive for several reasons: 1. These agencies are among the highest-priced vendors we use. 2. They already charge fees that our limited budgets cannot accommodate. 3. When they learn they have a semi monopoly on our business, they'll charge even more.	3. *An acknowledgment of the manager's point of view*
The freelancers and graphic design vendors I currently use are familiar with our technology; they do as good or better job than the agencies on the list, and their fees are reasonable.	4. *A request for a compromise solution*
I agree that reducing the number of agencies helps create a consistent look and strategy. But can we amend the new policy so that marketing	5. *A request for a response*

communications can continue to buy certain creative services on an a la carte basis? What do you think about this?

Sincerely,
(writer's name)

Model 4

Dear Danielle,

    I apologize for sending a Custom F-5 Module that was not produced according to your specifications. We have shipped a replacement unit that fits your specifications, via overnight freight, at our expense. It has been reviewed against your written specifications by Lanes Milstead, our senior application engineer. We'll arrange for someone to pick up the other unit — at our cost and your convenience, of course.

    Again, my apologies. We made a mistake, and I've alerted our production department to ensure that it is not repeated.

Sincerely,
(writer's name)

1. Apologize for the problem
2. Take responsibility
3. Show how the situation is now and will be prevented in the future

Useful Vocabulary and Expressions

Words

adjustment	inaccurate	misprint	resolve
compensation	inappropriate	misquote	slipshod
damaged	inconsistent	misrepresented	thoughtless
defective	inconvenient	nonfunctioning	uncooperative
dispute	insufficient	off-putting	unfortunate
dissatisfaction	lax	omission	unfounded
embarrassing	miscalculation	overcharged	unjustifiable
exasperating	misconception	overestimated	unpleasant
experience	misconstrued	overlooked	unprofessional
fault	mishandled	regrettable	unqualified
flaw	misinformed	reimburse	unreliable
grievance	misinterpreted	repay	unwarranted

Phrases

a mix-up in my order	correct your records
appealing to you for help	defective upon arrival
as a longtime customer	does not meet our performance standards
call to your immediate attention	expect to hear from you soon
has not met my expectations	not up to your usual high standards register

hope to resolve this problem it has come to my attention that it is with reluctance that I must inform you I was displeased/distressed/disturbed by I wish to be reimbursed for	a complaint about serious omission/problem under the conditions of the warranty would like credit for you have generally given us excellent service, but

Sentences

- Anything you can do to speed matters up/resolve this problem will be greatly appreciated.
- I am expecting the courtesy of a prompt reply.
- I am writing regarding my last bill, invoice # G4889, dated August 15, 2022.
- I expect an adjustment to be made as soon as possible.
- I'm confident that we can resolve this matter to our mutual satisfaction.
- I regret/am sorry to inform you of the following unpleasant situation.
- I will send a check for the balance as soon as I receive a corrected statement. I wish to receive credit on my account for this item.
- I would appreciate a telephone call from you about this situation.
- Please contact me within three business days to make arrangements for rectifying the situation.
- Thank you for your prompt assistance with this situation/problem.
- The most satisfactory solution for us would be for you to send us a replacement lamp and reimburse us for the cost of mailing the defective lamp back to you.
- This product has been unsatisfactory in several respects.

Exercises

I. Translate the following sentences into English.

1. 我知道你会希望不再发生这样的事件。

_____

2. 据我所知，维修/更换费用将由您承担。

_____

3. 我想退款 49.99 美元。

_____

4. 我想尽快澄清这一误解。

_____

5. 我们希望毫不拖延地解决这一难题。

II. Write a letter of Complaints based on the following condition.

File number: No. VF449766 of 4 July 1978

Complaints: Customer receives wrong goods. Case 14 is not sent as expected

Action: Arrange for replacements to be dispatched at once

III. Write a Response letter to a customer's complaints based on the following condition.

A woman purchased a particular flavor of ice cream and found that it did not have the usual amount of chocolate chips in it. Disappointed, she wrote the manufacturer to complain.

Response to customer's complaints:

Appreciation

Overview

Letters of appreciation are the easiest, most delightful letters to write. You are never obliged to write them, there is no deadline, and the only rule is sincerity. One of life's small pleasures is to be able to be kind and generous with little cost to yourself.

Letters of appreciation are related to letters of acknowledgment, congratulations, and thanks. In the latter cases, we are not surprised to hear from others, whereas a letter of appreciation is always unexpected.

You don't need to thank someone for prompting payment, for turning in a report, for giving you a bonus based on performance, or for returning your lost wallet intactly. In all these cases people are doing the expected thing. However, it is entirely appropriate to show your appreciation. Letters of appreciation are sent to employees who do "ordinary" work but do it well; to strangers you encounter who demonstrate above-average efficiency and service; to friends and relatives who go the extra mile for you; to people who have referred work or clients to you. Letters of Appreciation are written for: community service, customer referrals, customers whose business you want to acknowledge, employees for their good work, helpful advice/suggestions/tips, prompt payments, speeches/workshops/conferences.

Format

- State what you appreciate.
- Use a key word early in your note: "appreciation", "congratulations", "gratitude", "admiration", "recognition".
- Be specific about the person's work, talent, or actions.
- Close with wishes for continued success or with some forward-looking remarks about

your future business or personal association.

Models

Model 1

Mr. and Mrs. Barry White	*Purpose of the letter*
1876 Grampite Road Dottie, RI02804	
Dear Mr. and Mrs. White,	
I am writing to let you know about the client appreciation program I have instituted for people like you who are my most valued clients.	*Special services to valued customers*
Each month, I send out valuable tips and information about the real estate industry to this select group of people. You will receive articles on topics ranging from home budgeting and home remodeling to renouncing and home equity lines of credit.	*Reasons*
I am constantly trying to improve the level of service I provide because in my business your trust and respect are essential to my success.	
I will contact you soon to see how I might be able to help you meet any new real estate needs you might have.	*Close with forward-looking remarks about future business*
Yours sincerely,	
(writer's name)	

Model 2

Dear Ms. Lieb,	
Just a short note to express my appreciation for your courteous letter and for sending a replacement amplifier cover so promptly.	*Say "thank you" and explain why*
In today's pressured world, many customers (including myself) are quick to criticize and slow to praise. This is a letter of praise.	*Acknowledge that your complaint was addressed to your satisfaction*
Your response was fair and exactly what I wanted. You have resolved my problem, transformed dissatisfaction into satisfaction, and assured continued future orders from me. Both of us have got what we want.	
Thank you.	*Assure the recipient of future business*
Sincerely,	
(writer's name)	

    Whether you are a businessperson or a consumer, if your complaint is addressed and resolved, you should extend the courtesy of a letter of Appreciation. The key message of this letter is: "Your strategy worked; by resolving the problem as I requested, you retained me as a customer."

A well-written Letter of Appreciation carries a strong message. They give the recipient motivation to continue to please you in the future.

Model 3

Dear Mrs. Sixsmith,	
I wish to express my appreciation for accompanying the fifth and sixth graders to Language Camp last weekend. I understand you chaperoned the group on your own time. Since Ronald arrived home, I've heard dozens of stories of your helpfulness, good humor, and ability to make the camp a home-away-from-home for these youngsters.	*Mention the case* *Be specific about the person's work*
We felt a lot better knowing you would be with the group, and we appreciate Ronald's opportunity to spend time with a dynamic adult who's a good role model.	*Appreciate again*
With best wishes.	
<div align="right">Sincerely, (writer's name)</div>	

Useful Vocabulary and Expressions

Words

admire	honor	remarkable	thoughtfulness
appreciate	impressive	respect	thrilled
commendable	inspired	satisfying	touched
delightful	kindness	sensational	treasure
fascinating	knowledgeable	sincere	triumph
favorite	large-hearted	stunned	unique
generous	memorable	superb	welcome
gracious			

Phrases

appreciate your contributions to	I want you to know how much we/I appreciate your job
impressive inspired kindness	
as a token of our gratitude/appreciation	it was thoughtful of you to offer my compliments
grateful to you for	
delighted to learn about	realize the worth of
heard about your success	set great store by
held in high regard	think highly of
hope I can return the favor someday	we can point with pride
I am impressed by/with	without your dedication and expertise
important contribution	would like to compliment you on

Sentences

- Can you stand one more compliment?
- Customers like you are the reason we stay in business.
- I don't know how I would have managed without your help. If I can repay your kindness, let me know.
- I sincerely appreciate your time and attention.
- My hat's off to you!
- Thanks again for your clever and useful suggestion.
- The XXX School Board would like to add its thanks and appreciation to those of the recipients of the scholarships you made possible.
- We are all happy for you. Well done!
- Your efforts have made this possible. Your support is greatly appreciated. You've done it again!

Exercises

I. Translate the following sentences into English.

1. 作为杰罗姆小学的校长，你可能想知道，我们认为路易莎小姐是一个绝对的财富。

2. 我想对你在我接受旁路手术住院期间给予我的专业和富有同情心的照顾表示感谢。

3. 我想对你们所有人表示感谢，感谢你们上周为获得 HX 合同付出的额外时间和辛勤工作。

4. 我想告诉你，我非常感谢你为我们社区的垃圾回收工作所做的一切。

5. 过去的一年，对公司来说是重要的一年，你为公司的成功做出了重要贡献。

II. Write Letters of Appreciation on the conditions given.

1. For Ms. Stanley's superb workshop on hard disk filing system.

2. For Mr. Fitz's compliments to Ms. Stretton's outstanding service.

Refusal

Overview

When we have no interest in an activity and also have a solid excuse (being out of the country or out of money, for example), letters of refusal, regret, and rejection are easy to write.

To write letters of refusal (also known as regrets and rejections), be certain that you want to say "no", and ambivalence will weaken your letter. A good reason for saying "no" is simply "I don't want to". When you have a specific reason for saying no, you can give it. A Refusal is often written to say "No" to: adjustment/claims requests, employment, invitations, proposals, requests, sales, offers, and etc.

Format

- Thank the person for the offer, request, invitation.
- Make a courteous remark, agreeing with the person.
- Say "no" expressing your regret at having to do so.
- If you wish, explain your position.
- Suggest alternate courses of action or other resources, if appropriate.
- Close with a pleasant wish to be of more help next time.

Models

Model 1

Dear Mr. Quentin, 　　I would like to return Mr. MacIn's jacket to him, but I don't have it. 　　The jacket your trucker saw says, "I love Dale, Wes and Virginia." I had that jacket made specially for my wife. Those are our three children's names. I checked our register of truckers, and there was no Sam MacIn at our station on the Saturday you mentioned. Perhaps he was at Mrs. Rick's Mobile Station. The phone number there is 612-555-3827. People get us mixed up all the time. 　　I'm sorry I couldn't help you. I hope Mr. MacIn finds his jacket soon. 　　　　　　　　　　　　　　　　Sincerely, 　　　　　　　　　　　　　　　Cameron Mrstik	*Refusal* *Explanation* *Added Service* *Regret* *Goodwill*

Model 2

Dear Mr. Smith, 　　I am sure that you value having a good name with the investment community. I am surprised that you continue to send me payment notices, since I was offered a free trial of your newsletter. 　　I have repeatedly indicated that I have no interest in the Buying/Selling newsletter. I have repeatedly marked cancel on your invoices as your initial offer indicated. Enclosed, please find that original offer. As your offer indicates, "This will end the matter — with no cost to me." 　　Wouldn't it be embarrassed to learn that annoying collection letters were sent to individuals who took him at his word? 　　I expect this matter to end now. 　　　　　　　　　　　　　　　　Sincerely, 　　　　　　　　　　　　　　　　Kelly Jacobs	*Say why you do not owe the money* *Back up the statement with as much proof* *Express your annoyance* *Tell the reader what you expect to happen*

Model 3

Reasons for this refusal could be: You receive an enormous number of requests which you cannot give all. You may also want to say your budget for giving has been exceeded or already allocated for the year. Their requests came too late.

Dear Event Organizer, On behalf of the Michigan Islanders organization, thank you for your recent correspondence regarding the work of your organization and its ongoing need for support.	*Thanks for the requests.*
As you are aware, the Michigan Islanders views itself as more than just a professional franchise. We believe that our team is an integral part of the community and should participate in a variety of programs that touch the lives of all our residents. The club board reviews a broad spectrum of charitable requests that come to our attention. We grant requests up to a reasonable limit for only Michigan-based charities.	*Explain your position*
Regretfully, given the enormous number of daily requests we receive, the Islanders will be unable to provide your outstanding organization with a contribution at this time for we have reached our maximum donation limit. We are touched and honored, however, that you reached out to the team as you seek the additional resources that will enable you to move forward.	*Reasons for refusal*

Again, on behalf of everyone at the Michigan Islanders, thank you for your letter and our best wishes for a successful event.
                                      Sincerely,
                                      (writer's name)
	Close with good wish

Model 4

Dear Dean Arabin, I regret that I am unable to represent Barchester College at the inauguration of Dr. Eleanor Bold as the new president of Century College on September 16.	*Refusal*
I was unable to reschedule a previous commitment for that day.	*Reasons for refusal*

My wife is a graduate of Century, so I would have particularly enjoyed being part of the ceremony. Thank you for thinking of me. I was honored to be asked to represent the College and would be glad to be of service at some other time.
    I hope you are able to make other arrangements.
                                        Sincerely,
                                      (writer's name)
	Thanks with offer of further help

Useful Vocabulary and Expressions

Words

awkward	contraindicated	decline	difficult
dilemma	doubtful	impossible	impractical
obstacle	overextended	overstocked	regretfully
reject	reluctantly	respond	unable
unavailable	unfeasible	unfortunately	unlikely

Phrases

after much discussion/evaluation although the idea is appealing because of prior commitments company policy prohibits us from doesn't qualify/warrant due to present budget problems I appreciate you asking me, but I know how understanding you are, so normally I would be delighted, but not an option at the moment previous commitments regret to inform you your idea has merit, but	although I am sympathetic to beyond the scope of the present study current conditions do not warrant disinclined at this time decline/demur/pass up/withdraw I regret that I cannot accept it. It's a wonderful program, but puts me in something of a dilemma remain unconvinced of the value of sincerely regret unable to help/comply/grant/offer/provide

Sentences

- Although your entry did not win, we wish you good luck and many future successes.
- I don't think this will work for us.
- I have taken on more projects than I can comfortably handle.
- I know we'll be missing a wonderful time.
- I'm sorry not to be able to give you the reference you requested in your letter of November 3.
- I sympathize with your request and wish I could help.
- I wish I could be more helpful, but it's not possible now.
- I wish I didn't have to refuse you, but I'm not in a position to make the loan to you.
- Unfortunately, our present schedule is inflexible.
- The Board has, unfortunately, turned down your request.
- Unfortunately, this is not a priority for Pettifer Grains at this time.
- We are unable to approve your loan application at this time.

- We regret to say that a careful examination of your résumé does not indicate a particular match for our present needs.
- Your request comes at a particularly difficult time for me—I'm over-scheduled for the next two months.

Exercises

I. Translate the following sentences into English.

1. 虽然我们感谢您对 M&M 玩具的兴趣，但您的产品不是我们能够成功销售的产品。

2. 我很感激你的提议，但在我到公司之外寻求解决方案之前，我想先尝试一些事情。

3. 如果您重新阅读合同，特别是第 C1 条，您将看到我们在这方面没有法律义务。

4. 我希望这将帮助您理解为什么我们无法提供您要求的额外资金。

5. 我们已经审核了您的信用申请，很遗憾地通知您，目前我们无法向您提供银行卡。

II. Write letters of Refusal on the conditions given.

1. Request: direct the annual fund-raise.
   Reason of refusal: several other time-consuming commitments.

2. Case: Submission of a novel named "The Ninth Son" to the editors of BCD Review.
   Reason of refusal: The work is not suited to the current needs of the magazine.

Chapter 4

Research Paper

Thesis writing can be challenging for students and supervisors. The completion of a research paper, especially a PhD dissertation, involves mastery of a range of technical accomplishments, from learning an appropriate writing style to managing references, and from developing techniques for writing quickly to being effective at self-criticism and at criticizing the work of others.

This Chapter is divided into six units, each dealing with one section of a research article: Introduction, Literature Review, Methodology, Results and Findings, Discussion, Conclusion and Abstract. Since the aim of this Chapter is to enable you to write in a conventional way, each unit is designed to help you discover what the conventional model of that section of a research article looks like. In each unit, you will also be given support on the grammar and writing skills needed to write that section of the research article and you will be guided towards the appropriate vocabulary and expressions.

Introduce the Study

In this unit, we will be considering the opening chapter of a thesis. First, we will reflect on its purpose or functions and then look at the type of content that is typically presented and at ways in which it might be organized. The introductory chapter, or introduction, is the first part of an essay. It has two functions: (1) attracts the reader's interest, and (2) introduces the topic of the essay.

In order to help you write the Introduction to your own research, the model you build must reflect the following content:

1. Your introduction briefly discusses the historical developments of researches regarding the specific topic you are interested to study. What is important here is that you should be able to argue that your topic has a certain level of significance that warrants its study. However, if you argue that it has been fully studied, you will have to justify strongly why you are still studying it perhaps by pointing out the flaws in its development or in the literature (research gaps).

2. Describe the basic assumptions that lead you to study the topic. This should build up on the arguments you may have presented.

3. Justify why you think there is still a need to further study the topic. Your description of the historical development of researches related to the topic should help you in your justification. This is especially true if there are indications as highlighted by current knowledge that existing issues have not been fully studied and resolved, or that there are new issues that need to be studied.

4. Briefly describe how you intend to go about conducting the study. Is your study going to be an experiment, a case analysis, or a survey? This brief description should give

the reader an idea of how you intend to pursue the study. In other words, upon reading your introductory part, your readers may get to know why the topic is important and why there is a need to study it.

Guidance and Structure of Writing the Introductory Section

Introductions are crucial, and it speaks for you as you strive to join an international community of scholars. So, take some time to write the introduction properly and revise it on a regular basis as your research project matures.

The purpose of the first chapter of your thesis is to introduce your work. It consists of five brief components: Context of the Study, Statement of the Problem, Aim and Scope, Significance of the Study and, finally, an Overview.

1. Context of the Study

Before you begin talking about the problem, you must first provide some context to it. If you ignore this initial section, your readers may feel as if they have entered a conversation that has already started without them. The context of the study normally contains basic background information and assumptions that show the particular field or endeavor.

To make this point clear, here is a hypothetical example of how this section might be structured:

Context of the Study

Research worldwide indicates that there is a clear influence of membership in a social networking group within a multimedia organization in enhancing greater participation of organization members in the various operational activities of the organization (Amadeus, 2000). Studies in North America and Europe indicate that members of social networks, particularly tweeters are more active participants in performing activities required by their respective organizations (Forbes, 2006). In Asia, however, there is a dearth of empirically based information on this topic (Guzman, 2008). Hence, there is a distinct relationship between membership in a social network and the nature of performance in the operations of the organization.

In this example, we can clearly see that previous researches which are closely related to the present study are listed and intended to drive the readers to the proposed field—membership in social network and performance in the operations of the organization.

Of the many possible sources of inspiration that stimulate the research, responding to specific issues within an established result for research is perhaps the most common. By placing your work in this way, you immediately put your readers in dialogue with those in your field.

From the start, be aware of how your style of writing, your tone, and your use of key terms underpin your approach to research and provide you with an introduction to the research community. The best way to determine an appropriate style is simple: go to several top journals in your field and note the way that their contributors write. Imitate them.

2. Statement of the Problem

Now that you've drive your readers into your work, the next task is to motivate further interest in the area—typically by "stating the problem", because your research is nearly always an attempt to find a solution to a problem that you have identified. You believe that the present way of doing things is inadequate in some way, or that existing theory does not give explanation satisfactorily. Sometimes to call it a problem may be too strong. In this case you might choose a better description such as "motivation for the study". A clear understanding of what problem exists in the current literature is still the best way to identify potential research problems to work on.

What should be in it? Certainly not a full review of the literature, although there might be some reference to it, because the shortcomings in previous approaches to the area might be the justification for carrying out the work to be described. There's no standard way to write a statement of the problem. Here is an example from Phakiti Aek (2003).

Statement of the Problem (sample 1)

To date, there has not been sufficient research that examines the connection between actual strategy use and actual L2 language performance. If strategy use does indeed make a difference in L2 performance, it is equally important to understand the correlation between strategy use and L2 performance. In summary, if we could systematically add all the pieces of information derived from research onto characteristics of the testing procedures, test-takers background characteristics and strategy use, it would be quite intriguing to know the degree to which these factors accounted for language test performance and the extent to which language ability was actually tested.

From Chapter One: Introduction in Phakiti, Aek (2003).

Note that there is no review of literature or theory in Sample 1, merely a clear statement that here was a large problem that was worth putting some effort into — *"the degree to which these factors accounted for language test performance and the extent to which language ability was actually tested"*.

Also, there are some other examples, in which there is a review of literature, and the problem or gap of previous research was pointed out after the overview of literature.

Statement of the Problem (sample 2)

One way to toughen polymers is to incorporate a layer of rubber particles (Weimann et al, 2004) and there has been extensive research regarding the rubber modification of PLA. For example, Penney et al (2001) showed that PLA composites could be prepared using blending techniques and more recently, Hillier (2016) established the toughness of such composites. However, although the effect of the rubber particles on the mechanical properties of copolymer systems was demonstrated over two years ago (Deschf, 2017), little attention has been paid to the selection of an appropriate rubber component.

In the first sentence of sample 2, the writer provides a transition between the general problem area and the literature review. As a general rule, you should include references to previous or current research wherever it is useful, even in a sentence whose function is primarily to provide a transition.

In the second sentence, the writer provides a brief overview of key research projects in this area. You can't just "pour" the literature review onto the page in any order; you should arrange your references and studies so that the reader is able to process them in a logical way. Here are three common options:

- **Chronological:** Deal with the research in chronological order may be appropriate, for example, if the development of your eld is related to political decisions.
- **Different approaches/theories/models:** Group projects or studies according to their approach or methodology. Grouping similar projects together helps you avoid the "tennis match" effect where you go backwards and forwards, beginning each sentence in the literature review with However or On the other hand.
- **General/specific:** Start with general research in the eld and gradually move to research that is closer to your own.

In the third sentence, the writer describes a gap in the research, which states the problem of research.

Grounded in a context, the statement of the problem sets out the reason the research is worth tackling. In summary, a "Statement of the Problem" or "Motivation for the Study" generally contains four parts:

- A brief history of the issue at hand.
- A recent increase of the issue.
- Dissatisfaction with current knowledge.
- An identification of specific research problem.

3. Aim and Scope of the Study

This is where you begin to introduce the purpose of your paper and the specific problem you will deal with, and in order to do this, it is necessary to create a research scope. You can do this either by describing a problem in the previous research or by indicating that there is a gap in the research. It is conventional to introduce it with a signaling expression such as However or Although. In professional writing it is unusual to put it in the form of a question; instead, you can state it as a prediction or a hypothesis which you intend to test. At this stage you move to the present work. You can describe it, say what its purpose or focus is.

Don't be shy about pointing out the problems in previous research. In the first place it may be necessary in order to explain why you have done your study, and in the second place, the language used here is usually respectful and impersonal, and is therefore not considered offensive. We will look at the aspect of politeness of this language in the vocabulary section at the end of the unit.

Aim of the study

However, although the effect of the rubber particles on the mechanical properties of copolymer systems was demonstrated over two years ago, little attention has been paid to the selection of an appropriate rubber component. The present paper presents a set of criteria for selecting such a component.

Your stated aim should have three characteristics:

- It should follow as a logical consequence of the problem statement. You identify a problem, and your aim is to address it; as just noted, you have to be clear about what the problem is.
- It should be singular. You must identify only one aim.
- The conclusions in your last chapter must respond to this aim. Over the months you work on your thesis, it is easy to forget the relationship of the introduction and the final conclusion. When you have written the last sentence of your conclusions, go back and re-read your aim. If the conclusions don't respond to the aim, you had better rewrite it; and don't forget, you will also need to rewrite the problem statement that leads up to it.

You will need to think critically at each stage of your work. To start the process of being critical, you must first set limits. A major part of being critical is to be able to set the terms of your debate and focus on what is particularly relevant to your aim.

In some areas of study, the scope of the investigation might require only a few sentences. In others, especially newly developing areas, it might require an elaborate discussion. Here is an example of a scope.

Scope of the study

Limits to the research are noted from the start. I do not, for example, examine the learners' listening development in interactional listening environments. The research is narrowed down to an emphasis on one-way, or transactional listening. The research is also focused on listening as an audio-based skill where no visual elements are presented. The study additionally focuses on "learning to listen" rather than "listening to learn" (Rost 2002; Vandergrift 2004). In other words, the emphasis is on learning how to improve one's listening ability rather than using listening as a vehicle to acquire the language. There is a need for these limitations because the investigation of listening comprehension processes and instruction is such a complex area.

In the study, I also limit the participants to native Mandarin Chinese-speaking EFL learners in Taiwan, China. I choose learners in an EFL rather than an English as a second language (ESL) context, because this EFL environment is more likely to minimize the influences on the listeners' development outside the classroom environment, therefore providing a clearer insight into probable developmental effects associated with the instruction. Native Chinese-speaking learners are chosen because of the considerable distance between the English and Chinese languages, as English is a stress-timed language and Chinese is a tone language. This distance between the languages is especially pronounced in terms of the phonological differences between the two languages, which have been found to present major challenges for Chinese learners of English (Brown and Hilferty 1986; Pennington and Ellis 2000).

If you set out your limits, you are more likely to finish the thesis, and most importantly, your examiners will be impressed that they have in hand a focused, high-impact study.

4. Significance of the Study

A way to think of the significance of your thesis is to connect it with the potential impact: Where do you think your study will make the most difference to current thinking? There are four lines of argument that may be used to establish the significance of a study.

- First, it may create new knowledge (for example, the results will extend what is known about the applicability of a theory, the results are widely generalizable, etc.).
- Second, a study may contribute to the solution of a practical problem faced by many others in the field.
- Third, it may demonstrate a novel use of a procedure or technique.
- Fourth, a study may contribute to part of a programmatic research effort; that is, when the results of the study are considered in relation to other studies, there may be theoretical or practical applications of major proportions.

Each line of argument that is applicable should be pursued. Let's take a look at an example to see how the author wrote about the significance.

Significance of study

One intended outcome of the study, on a theoretical level, is to identify a preliminary set of learner factors that arise out of extended exposure to two different approaches on the development of second language listening behaviors. On a practical level, a second intended outcome of the study is to clarify research techniques to do with the investigation of listening abilities. Specifically, I focus on Chinese learners of English at lower proficiency levels. Further, a third intended outcome contributes to the design of listening instruction by articulating a set of multi-level course design guidelines tailored for individual differences, particularly those associated with learner listening style. Evidence from reading and listening research supports this need to include both of these dimensions of listening proficiency and listening style in such a set of guidelines; findings from various studies (Davis and Bistodeau 1993; Vandergrift 1998a, b) have suggested the significant impact that both factors may have on learner response to differing forms of instruction relevant to the "top-down/bottom-up debate". Finally, a further concern in the research is the sequencing of skills and strategies for learners through a listening course.

5. Overview of the Study

The overview of the study should be written in the form of interconnected sentences and paragraphs to ensure that the logic flow is clear to the reader. Here is an example of an overview of a study. Look at the example below:

Overview of the study

This thesis consists of seven further chapters within three main parts. In PART I (Chap. 2 & 3), I situate the current study in related literature and establish the research methodology. In Chap. 2, I discuss the theoretical underpinnings of language and culture to guide the enquiry. Chap. 3 deals with the methodological issues and research design providing the philosophical foundations, case study context (i.e. SA), theoretical and procedural description of instruments used in the study to collect, present, and analyze data. In PART II (Chap. 4, 5, & 6), I present the results of data analysis of the place of FC in policy, instructors' practice, and pre-service teachers' EFL learning respectively. PART III (Chap. 7 & 8) contains the discussion, recommendations, and conclusions of the current study.

The researcher uses overview of the study to describe the approach used in the whole project—which will include historical reviews, reviews of theory and practice, accounts of the researcher's own work, and synthesis of all of these to permit conclusions to be drawn.

6. Research Questions and Hypotheses

A general statement of the research questions or a hypothesis should be made in the first chapter, or alternatively, make sure these are clear in the statement of your aim. Otherwise, readers may struggle to understand what the point of the thesis is.

The research questions can be generated after an area is reviewed and gaps are identified. Accordingly, the right place for a precise statement of the research questions may be at the point where the background chapters finish, but the questions need to be stated in broad terms in your first chapter.

A hypothesis is a proposition made as a starting point for further investigation from known facts. The first chapter of a thesis could also be an extensive review of the literature ending up with a research hypothesis. Your first mention of the word hypothesis should be in the chapter concerned with your own work. When you do use it, stick to its formal meaning. You should be able to deduce from the combination of your review of current theory and practice, and possibly from your own preliminary studies, that there are certain lines of thought that are worth investigating by careful tests. They will tell you without doubt whether your hypothesis has stood up or whether it has been demolished.

Summary of the Introductory Section

Your introductory chapter should consist of five elements:

1. *Context of the Study*
— Provide a brief history of the issues to date.
— Situate your particular topic within the broad area of research.

2. *Problem statement*
— Identify a key point of concern.
— Refer to the literature to demonstrate why your project is worth doing.
— Be sure that the motivation, or problem, suggests a need for further investigation.

3. *Aim and Scope*
— Be sure that your aim responds logically to the problem statement.
— Stick rigorously to a single aim.
— When you have written the conclusions to your whole study, check that they respond to this aim.
— Be sure to establish the scope of your study by identifying limitations of factors such as time, location, resources, or the established boundaries of particular fields or theories.

4. *Significance of the Study*
— Explain how your thesis contributes to the field.
— There are four main areas of contribution: theory development, tangible solution, innovative methods, and policy extension. One of these contributions must be identified as the basis of your primary contribution to the field.

5. *Overview of the Study*
— Sketch out how the thesis is structured. Don't confine yourself to a list of chapters but show how they are linked, and that one section logically leads to another.

— Check whether the reader can see from this sketch how the aim will be achieved.

Vocabulary and Sentence Pattern for the Introduction Section

1. Expressions for Establishing Significance

	(has been) extensively studied
(a) basic issue	numerous investigations
(a) central problem	of great concern
(a) challenging area	of growing interest
(a) classic feature	one of the best-known
(a) common issue	over the past ten years
(a) current problem	play a key role (in)
(a) dramatic increase	play a major part (in)
(a) fundamental issue	potential applications
(a) growth in popularity	recent decades
(a) key technique	well-documented
(a) leading cause (of)	well-known
(a) major issue	widely recognized
(a) popular method	widespread
(a) powerful tool/method	worthwhile
(a) rapid rise	attracted much attention
(a) vital aspect	benefit/beneficial
(a) worthwhile study	commercial interest
	during the past two decades

Here are some examples of how these are used:

- **A major current focus** in population management is how to ensure the sustainability of...

- **Numerous experiments have established that** radiation causes...

- ... have **generated considerable recent research interest.**

- Analysis of change in the transportation sector is **vital** for two **important** reasons: ...

- **It is generally accepted that** joints in steel frames operate in a semi-rigid fashion.

- Nanocrystalline oxide films **are attracting widespread interest** in elds.

- These phenomena **play an important role in** the development of...

- For **more than 100 years** researchers have been observing the stress-strain behavior of...

- **Much research in recent years has focused on** carbon nanotubes.

2. Gap/Question/Problem/Criticism

ambiguous	not dealt with	(the) next step
confused	not repeatable	(an) obstacle
deficient	not studied	(a) weakness
doubtful	of little value	(to) demand clarification
expensive	over-simplistic	(to) disagree
far from perfect	problematic	(to) fail to
ill-defined	questionable	(to) fall short of
impractical	redundant	(to) miscalculate
inaccurate	restricted	(to) misunderstand
inadequate	time-consuming	(to) need to re-examine
incompatible (with)	unresolved	(to) neglect
inconclusive	unsupported (the) absence of	(to) overlook
inconsistent	(a) challenge	(to) remain unstudied
ineffective	(a) defect	(to) require clarification
inferior	(a) difficulty	(to) suffer (from)
inflexible	(a) disadvantage	few studies have...
insufficient	(a) drawback	it is necessary to...
meaningless	(a) flaw	little evidence is available
misleading	(a) gap in our knowledge	little work has been done
non-existent	(a) lack	more work is needed
not addressed	(a) limitation	there is growing concern
not apparent	(a) need for clarification	there is an urgent need...

Here are some examples of how these are used:

- **Few researchers have addressed the problem** of ...

- **There remains a need for** an efficient method that can...

- However, light scattering techniques have been **largely unsuccessful**...

- The high absorbance makes this **an impractical option** in cases where...

- **Unfortunately,** these methods do not always guarantee...

- **An alternative approach** is necessary.

- The function of these proteins **remains unclear.**

- These can be **time–consuming** and are often **technically difficult** to perform.

- **Although** this approach improves performance, it results in **an unacceptable** number of ...

- Previous work has focused **only** on ...

- However, the experimental configuration was **far from optimal.**

3. The Present Work

(to) facilitate (to) illustrate (to) improve (to) manage to (to) minimize (to) outline (to) predict (to) present (to) propose (to) provide (to) reveal (to) succeed	(this) work begin by/with close attention is paid to overview	simple straightforward successful valuable
		aim goal intention objective purpose

Here are some examples of how these are used:

- **This paper focuses on** ...
- **The purpose of this study is to describe and examine...**
- **In order to** investigate the biological significance...
- **In this paper we present...**
- New correlations were developed with **excellent** results...
- **In the present study** we performed...
- **This paper introduces** a scheme which solves these problems.
- **The approach we have used in this study** aims to...
- **This study** investigated the use of ...
- **In this report** we test the hypothesis that...
- **This paper is organized as follows:** ...

Exercises

I. A short essay is composed of the three parts of introduction, body and conclusion. The introduction part plays an important role in academic writing. It's important to know how to write an introduction for a research paper.

Discuss the following questions with your partner.

1. Why do we need to write an introduction for the paper?
2. What is the structure of an introduction in academic writing?
3. How do we define the terms and concepts in the introduction?

II. Read the text and finish the following writing tasks.

Anticipating acceptance of emerging technologies using twitter: the case of self-driving cars

Christopher Kohl1 · Marlene Knigge1 · Galina Baader1 · Markus Böhm1 ·

Introduction

1. The evolution of transportation has faced numerous trials as it has grown and expanded over time. It seems safe to assume that this steady chain of development of faster and safer vehicles with improved technological features continues (e.g., Burns 2013). Over the past decade, a vast amount of research has been conducted regarding the topic of self-driving cars (Fagnant and Kockelman 2015; Kyriakidis et al. 2015), which are being vigorously pursued by companies in the automotive and related industries. Even native IT companies such as Google are pursuing the development of self-driving cars (Spinrad 2014). However, for a technology to be successful, we must remember a significant key factor for the success of emerging technologies, technology acceptance (Davis et al. 1989).

2. In recent years, self-driving cars have become a controversially discussed topic. Ethical, regulatory, and liability concerns (Zmud and Sener 2017; Gogoll and Müller 2017), centering on who is driving and who assumes responsibility for accidents, are hotly debated issues. Nevertheless, the automotive and related industries seem convinced that self-driving cars will be the future of mobility and may underestimate the public's concerns and misconceptions related to this emerging technology (Piao et al. 2016) that often differ from the perceptions of experts (Blake 1995). With the first intelligent vehicle handling systems, a pre-stage of technologies that enable self-driving cars, Conover (1994) already discussed that risk and benefit perceptions could be an issue. Research regarding other technologies also shows that risk and benefit perceptions are central determinants of their public acceptance (Siegrist 2000; Butakov and Ioannou 2015). Public perceptions, therefore, eventually determine whether self-driving cars will be used and, thus, are a crucial factor that needs to be considered especially for initial acceptance of emerging technologies such as self-driving cars (Butakov and Ioannou 2015; Pendleton et al. 2015;Bansal et al. 2016).

3. However, studies addressing public perception and acceptance of this emerging technology, especially across several countries and its change over time, remain scarce. We address this paucity of research by first outlining the results of previous research on public perception and acceptance of self-driving cars. Second, we describe a new approach to measure and react to public perceptions facilitating the voice of the customer (VOC). This approach gives us the opportunity to utilize the vast amounts of data publicly available in social media to anticipate acceptance of emerging technologies and answer the following

research questions:

RQ1: How can we measure public perceptions of self-driving cars to anticipate acceptance?

RQ2: How do events influence the public perception of self-driving cars?

4. To address these research questions, we create an approach for automatically determining and monitoring perceived risks and benefits of emerging technologies from short 140-character text messages published on the social media platform Twitter. We build on scientific literature and text mining methods, which allow the extraction of knowledge from text documents (Tan 1999) and, more specifically, sentiment analysis (Hopkins and King 2010). We use the social media platform Twitter to collect a stream of opinions about self-driving cars, one instance of currently emerging technology. Based on the perceived risks and benefits of self-driving cars, we identify events and issues crucial for the future acceptance of this emerging technology and guide the management of emerging technologies.

5. The remainder of this paper is structured as follows: First, we provide an overview of current literature on technology acceptance, self-driving cars, and previous research on the acceptance of self-driving cars. Second, we describe the data extraction from Twitter, the preprocessing of the data, and the model generation including its evaluation. Third, we describe and discuss the results of extracting the relevant data and applying our machine learning model to this data. We conclude with a summary of the results, limitations of our work, possibilities for further research, and the contributions to research and practice.

Task One *Read the introduction of a paper and answer the following questions.*

1. How does the author introduce the research topic?

2. Have self-driving cars been accepted by the general public and scholars in transportation?

3. What are the research questions involved in the paper?

4. What is the methodology employed in the research?

5. How is the paper structured?

Task Two *Read the introduction again and find what information is needed in the introduction part. Match the paragraph number with the elements listed in the box below.*

| Background/context   contribution   methodology   previous studies |
purpose   definition   outline

Para.1 _____

Para.2 _____

Para.3 _____

Para.4 _____
Para.5 _____

III. Write an Introduction.

A good introduction to prepare the reader for the body of writing that comes after it. It can be a thread of an idea that will follow through your paper. The purpose of the introduction is to introduce the background or context of the paper, describe the problems that will be addressed in the paper, briefly mention of previous studies relevant to the research topic, and then outline the main points the paper would cover.

Task One Read the following introduction part and match each sentence with an introduction element.

	In this sentence, the writer:
1. Polylactide (PLA) has received much attention in recent years due to its biodegradable properties, which offer important economic benefits.	1 _____
2. PLA is a polymer obtained from corn and is produced by the polymerization of lactide.	2 _____
3. It has many possible uses in the biomedical eld[1] and has also been investigated as a potential engineering material.[2,3]	3 _____
4. However, it has been found to be too weak under the impact to be used commercially.[4]	4 _____
5. One way to toughen polymers is to incorporate a layer of rubber particles[5] and there has been extensive research regarding the rubber modification of PLA.	5 _____
6. For example, Penney et al. showed that PLA composites could be prepared using blending techniques[6] and more recently, Hillier established the toughness of such composites.[7]	6 _____
7. However, although the effect of the rubber particles on the mechanical properties of copolymer systems was demonstrated over two years ago,[8] little attention has been paid to the selection of an appropriate rubber component.	7 _____
8. The present paper presents a set of criteria for selecting such a component.	8 _____
9. On the basis of these criteria it then describes the preparation of a set of polymer blends using PLA and a hydro-carbon rubber (PI).	9 _____
10. This combination of two mechanistically distinct polymerizations forms a novel copolymer in which the incorporation of PI significantly increases flexibility.	10 _____

Task Two *Write an introduction to an essay by answering the questions below.*

a) Which terms might need defining?

b) What background information could you give?

c) How about the studies by other writers who have discussed this topic.

d) What is your purpose in writing and the importance of the public transport?

e) How will you organize the main body of the essay?

Imagine that you have just completed a research project to design a bicycle cover which can protect the cyclist from injury, pollution, or just rain. Write the Introduction of your research paper entitled **A Cover for the SPPPV (Single-Person Pedal-Powered Vehicle)**, and your Introduction should be between 200~400 words. You can create as much as you like, and of course you will have to create fake research references. Follow the model as closely as possible; make sure your Introduction contains the four main components of the model and try out some of the new vocabularies.

Develop Literature Review

The aim of the literature review is to provide an in-depth account of the background literature relevant to the context that your study is located in and, in doing so, to provide an argument, case or justification for the study.

In fact, in preparing your thesis, the review of the literature is perhaps the first task you need to do. Then what is the review of the literature? A review of the literature is an "account of what has been published on a topic by accredited scholars and researchers" (http://en.wikipedia.org), which means that the review of the related literature is a synthesis of the published materials about a particular research topic (http://www.writing.utoronto.ca). Implied in this description or definition is the idea that a comprehensive review of the literature would greatly help determine the research gaps in the area of the study, as well as provide a synthesis of the latest developments in the discipline. This is the reason why researchers would be interested in how other researchers treat the literature related to their studies. These issues are discussed in more detail through this unit.

Guidelines and Structure of Literature Review

It is not necessary to review all the literature in the field especially if you are dealing with only a specific research topic. For example, much of the research literature in environmental science will be unnecessary in a specific study about climate change. What you need are materials that have direct relevance to the study you are going to conduct, i.e., reports of changes in weather patterns in selected areas of the country, changing rainfall patterns in various countries of the region, updated information of melting glaciers and ice caps, etc. What you are expected to review are only those that have relation to your study. The trick is to learn to discriminate what information may help you in your research and what information may be irrelevant. The review of related literature is an extremely important part of your thesis. In fact, in many cases, it is probably the most publishable part of your thesis. And the review of related literature is normally about 25 percent of the entire thesis.

Why do you have to review the related literature? The five basic purposes of the literature review are as follows:

1. The literature review expands the introductory chapter of your thesis, and normally helps in determining the research gaps in the particular area of interest that is addressed by the thesis.

2. The literature review helps to further define the research problem. Frequently, you will rea-lize that the literature review has partially answered your research questions.

3. The literature review provides the background and a clear discussion of the theoretical basis for your research (thesis) problem.

4. The literature review will help you interpret the results of your study.

5. The literature review will help you outline the implications of your study.

There are three basic elements which constitute the structure of a literature review:

• Introduction: to introduce the central theme and the organizational pattern.

• Body: to discuss and organize the sources.

• Conclusions: to illustrate the findings and relate them to your own research.

And there are two important strategies for writing the literature review: to summarize and to synthesize. To summarize means to summarize important information (arguments and ideas) of other researchers. To synthesize means to analyze and compare the literature in order to find out the different ways researchers have treated the topic, establish the connections between the sources, and illustrate how this past work fits together to make your research question significant.

Now, by the analysis of one example of the literature review part of a thesis, you can see how to write this part in a practical way:

Sample of Literature Review	**Functions of Sentence:**
(1) The reason for the increased emphasis on ESP is that it is recognized as a learner-centered approach to language instruction. (2) It is distinguished from other approaches by "a commitment to the goal of providing language instruction that addresses students' own specific purposes" (Belcher, 2009:2). (3) For a long time, English teaching in China has been criticized for producing low output with high input.	(1) Topic sentence (2) Further explanation to the topic sentence by quoting sparingly

(4) It is generally accepted that successful learning is crucially dependent on motivation (Ellis, 1997). (5) Chinese students complain that, despite assurances of the usefulness of English, after studying English and passing examinations for at least ten years, they have gained little from College English classes (Fan, 2013). (6) This greatly reduces their motivation. (7) **_By contrast_**, involvement with academic subjects in ESP prioritizes learners' needs and makes them aware of the practical value of English, thus increasing their motivation. (8) Strevens (1988) summarizes the advantages of ESP: being focused on the learner's needs, it wastes no time; is relevant to the learner; is successful in imparting learning; and thus, is more cost-effective than "general English".	(3) Synthesis of ideas to support the topic sentence (4) & (5) Summary of other researches provides evidence for the sentence "By contrast", which shows the structure of this paragraph follows a "comparison and contrast" order (7) Synthesis (8) Summary

Vocabulary and Sentence Patterns for the Literature Review

Expressions for Presenting Previous or Current Research

achieve	conclude	investigate
address	deal with	measure
adopt	debate	observe
analyze	demonstrate	prefer
apply	describe	obtain
argue	determine	overcome
assume	discover	perform
attempt	enhance	predict
carry out	estimate	propose
choose	focus on	publish
claim	generate	put forward
classify	identify	recommend
collect	illustrate	show
concentrate (on)	implement	simulate
	imply	

Here are some examples of how these are used:

- This phenomenon **was demonstrated** by...
- In their study, expanded T-cells **were found** in...

- Initial attempts **focused on identifying** the cause of...
- Weather severity **has been shown to**...
- Early data **was interpreted** in the study by...
- The algorithm **has been proposed** for these applications...
- The results on pair dispersion **were reported in**...
- Their study **suggested** a possible cause for...
- An alternative approach **was developed** by...

Common Errors in Reviewing the Scientific Literature

There are two common errors which are commonly commit when reviewing the literature related to the studies. These are:

- Too frequently, thesis writers rely solely on secondary materials or sources, or simply copy someone else's review of the literature. This could have serious consequences because there is a chance that the reviewer you may be referring to might have interpreted the original material differently from the way it should be. And plagiarism might be committed by cutting and pasting what is available. It is always wise to refer to the original material and properly cite it in the study.
- Very frequently, researchers concentrate on the findings in research reports. This is a serious error because if you look at the findings alone, you are likely to be misled by impressive statistics. The important parts of the research reports that you must analyze critically are the over-all methodology, sampling, research design and methods of analyses. It is a mistake to read only the results reported.

Exercises

I. In an earlier lecture, we have discussed some of the issues encountering in searching for information and selecting a valuable topic for a research project and the development of these into a research proposal. Innovation and creation of new knowledge grows through a process of accumulation, so we need to review the relevant literature to have a good understanding of the background knowledge. Just as Isaac Newton said, "If I can see further, it's because I am standing on the shoulders of giants."

Discuss the following questions with your partner.

1. What is literature review?
2. Why do we need to conduct a literature review in a research?
3. What are the components of a literature review?
4. What strategies can we use when developing a literature review?

II. Find out the Synthesis and Summary parts from the following literature review paragraphs.

1. Family-school cooperation has been emphasized, valued, and implemented for years in the Chinese mainland. For instance, home visits and parent-teacher group meeting are traditional and common ways of parent-teacher contacts (Li & Liu, 2011; Liu, 2010; Wang, 2008; Zhu, 2010). As well, with the fast development of science and technology, besides traditional ways of family-school contacts like home visits or telephone calls, many new ways like family-school communicating platform based on social networking services (e.g., Wechat or QQ) appeared (Di, 2016; Huang, 2016).

2. Learner autonomy refers to the learners' sense of responsibility for their learning and their ability to be responsible for what they learn (Dickinson, 1987; Holec, 1981). Thus, autonomous learners are those who take an active approach to the learning task and are willing to communicate in the target language by taking risks. Earlier studies by Holec (1981) and Dickinson (1995) have demonstrated that successful foreign language acquisition depends on learners taking responsibility for their own learning. More recently, book on the European Language Portfolio from Little et al. (2008) states that learner autonomy should also be an important goal of language instruction because not only does it motivate learning, it also serves as a pre-requisite for lifelong learning.

3. LTE theorists such as Graves (2009), Richards (2010), and Roberts (1998) distinguish multiple categories of teacher knowledge believed to be necessary for effective classroom performance. Subject matter knowledge, for example, entails explicit familiarity with instructional methods, learning theories, and language structure. Pedagogical content knowledge, in contrast, includes familiarity with curriculum development, teaching methods, and classroom management. Procedural knowledge (or skill) involves a teacher's repertoire of technical competencies, such as lesson planning, pedagogical reasoning, observational strategies, and the like (Borg, 2006; Graves, 2009; Hedgcock, 2009; Richards, 2008, 2010; Roberts, 1998). Some controversy in LTE surrounds the relative value of these knowledge categories and their rightful role in LTE (Chappell & Moore, 2012; Freeman, 1994; Freeman & Johnson, 2004; Hedgcock, 2002; Johnson, 2009; Yates & Muchisky, 2003). Further disagreement involves what should constitute suitable pedagogical content knowledge (Richards, 2010). Although these debates continue, LTE curricula typically identify some combination of these sources of knowledge and skill as appropriate goals for language teachers (Liu & Berger, 2015).

III. Reading Practice: Read the text and finish the following writing tasks.

Emotional Eating: The Perpetual Cycle of Mood–Food Influence

Abby Hurd

October 20, 2013

Introduction

1. It is no secret that obesity is a major health concern in the U.S., and stress and other negative emotions may be contributing to the problem. There has been much research on how the food we eat affects our physical health, but comparatively little research on the relationship between our eating behavior and emotional states. Studies have found that there is some science behind the tendency to drown our sorrows in a pint of Ben & Jerry's (Oliver & Wardle, 1999; Epel, Lapidus, McEwen, & Brownell, 2001). Research has also highlighted gender differences in the ways men and women use eating to cope with stress (Christensen & Brooks, 2006). The relationship between food and mood runs in the reverse direction as well, as eating behavior appears to have some bearing on subsequent moods: higher consumption of calories, saturated fat, and sodium are associated with negative moods one to two days later (Hendy, 2012). While increased consumption of "comfort foods", such as chocolate, ice cream, and potato chips, may provide temporary relief from stress and other negative emotions, these effects appear to wear off, perpetuating a cycle of stress-eating, which can lead over time to obesity (Dallman, Pecoraro, & la Fleur, 2005; Tomiyama, Dallman, & Epel, 2011). Research has shown that the relationship between food and mood is bidirectional: our moods can influence the type and quantity of food we consume, while the food we consume can in turn influence our later moods and, in some cases of chronic stress, lead to obesity and a dampening of the chronic stress response network.

Influence of Mood on Eating Behavior

2. Our emotional states play a significant role in the quantity and types of food we choose to eat. Studies have looked at the self-reported eating behaviors of male and female undergraduate college students in response to stress. One such study administered questionnaires to participants, assessing their beliefs about the effects of stress on their eating behavior (Oliver & Wardle, 1999). The results showed that about equal numbers of participants reported that they would increase their overall food intake when under stress (42%) and decrease their overall food intake when under stress (37%). Most of the participants (73%) reported increased consumption of snack-type foods when under stress (Oliver & Wardle, 1999). Thus, it appears that stress does have some effect on eating behavior. A possible explanation for these trends is that snack-type foods, such as sweets and chocolate, are calorically dense and quick to eat, making them a convenient choice when

we are under stress and do not have much time to eat. These snack-type foods also boost levels of the neurotransmitter serotonin, which improves mood and relieves stress (Oliver & Wardle, 1999). Thus, individuals may be drawn to snack-type foods as a way to self-medicate against their stress.

3. There are some areas of this research in need of more explanation, however. Oliver & Wardle's (1999) research report does not offer a clear operational definition of stress as defined in the questionnaires. There are many different ways to measure stress and varying degrees of stress, so it would be helpful to know how stress was defined in this study. Furthermore, this study is limited in its implications because it only assesses participants' beliefs about their eating behavior when under stress; it does not measure their actual behavior. Thus, we cannot be certain that the participants' self-reported eating behaviors in response to hypothetical stress accurately represent what they would actually eat in response to real-life stress, as actions do not always follow beliefs.

4. Another study looked at the effects of acute stress on eating behavior in pre-menopausal women aged 30~45 years. Participants completed both stressful and non-stressful tasks in separate sessions in a lab. After each session, they were exposed to snacks, and experimenters measured their food intake. Their levels of salivary cortisol, a stress hormone, were measured before the task, during the task, and afterwards (Epel et al., 2001). The results showed that participants with higher salivary cortisol levels consumed more total calories and more sweet, high-fat snacks following the stressful tasks, and more sweet snacks following both the stressful and non-stressful tasks (Epel et al., 2001). Cortisol release in response to stress may increase appetite and drive us to consume more food and show preference for sweet and high-fat foods (Epel et al., 2001). Thus, higher cortisol levels may increase individuals' vulnerability to stress-induced overeating.

Gender Differences

5. Further research has found differences between men and women in the perceived effects of mood on eating behavior. One study looked at male and female undergraduate college students' self-reported predicted eating behaviors in response to imaginary situations designed to make them feel happy or sad (Christensen & Brooks, 2006)...[sentences omitted] ... Women report more food cravings than do men, which could explain why women report specifically increasing their consumption of sweet, high-fat, high-carbohydrate foods in response to sad events. Women may be more likely to consume serotonin-boosting foods high in sugar, fat, and carbohydrates as a coping mechanism for dealing with distressing emotions such as sadness, while men may use other mechanisms, such as exercise, to cope with distress (Christensen & Brooks, 2006).

6. Oliver and Wardle (1999) found that both women and dieters report consuming more snack-type foods, such as sweets and chocolate, in response to stress than do men and non-dieters. Women and dieters may be more likely to restrict their eating when not under stress out of concern for body image ... [sentences omitted] ... In contrast, men who are not dieting likely do not restrict their eating as much when not under stress, and may not feel the need or desire to increase their consumption of high-calorie foods when under stress. In contrast, they may see happy moods as a more suitable occasion to increase food consumption, which would support the findings of Christensen and Brooks (2006).

Influence of Eating Behavior on Later Moods

7. The relationship between food and mood appears to run in the opposite direction as well: the food we consume affects our later moods. This has been shown in a study looking at the sequential relationship between food and mood over a seven-day period of undergraduate college students' everyday lives (Hendy, 2012). This study was able to show the effects of eating behavior on students' later moods in the context of the natural, day-to-day stressors they experienced. The results showed that negative moods tended to be reported one to two days after consuming higher amounts of calories, saturated fat, and sodium, while the associations between food consumption and positive moods were less consistent (Hendy, 2012).These findings suggest that stress-induced eating may be a perpetual, vicious cycle. When we eat foods higher in calories, saturated fat, and sodium in the presence of stress, these foods may give us temporary relief, but leave us feeling stress and other negative emotions one or two days later. This drives us to consume more of these types of food in an attempt to relieve our negative emotions, continuing the cycle. Over time, this can lead to weight gain and obesity.

Chronic Stress Response Network

8. Stress-induced eating can perpetuate a cycle of negative moods and increased consumption of high-calorie comfort foods, and this can have negative health consequences over time. Dampening of the chronic stress response network has been shown to play a role in the development of obesity over time in those who experience chronic stress (Dallman et al., 2005; Tomiyama et al., 2011). The chronic stress response network is regulated by the hypothalamo-pituitary-adrenal axis (HPA), and involves the hormones and brain systems that are activated in response to stress (Dallman et al., 2005). Experiments have demonstrated that rats exposed to stress initially show high levels of secretion of the stress hormone corticosterone, which is associated with food-related drives (Dallman et al., 2005) ... [sentences omitted] ... Their chronic stress response networks were stimulated to release lower levels of corticosterone and other stress hormones because the comfort foods these rats consumed were doing most of the job of providing stress relief (Dallman et al., 2005).

9. This muting of the chronic stress response network has been reported in humans as well. In a study that looked at 59 premenopausal women, those who were chronically stressed (as defined by the Perceived Stress Scale) showed lower levels of cortisol secretion than those who were not chronically stressed, indicating diminished HPA activity (Tomiyama et al., 2011)... [sentences omitted]... These findings suggest that chronic stress can lead to increased consumption of comfort foods, dampened HPA activity, and obesity, as individuals engage in a cycle of emotional eating as a way to self-medicate against their stress, in response to muted chronic stress response networks.

10. There are some limits, however, to the findings of these studies. The study (Tomiyama et al. 2011) on premenopausal women and chronic stress did not test the chronically stressed participants' levels of HPA activity at a point in their lives when they were not chronically stressed... [sentences omitted]... Thus, we cannot make definite conclusions about the direction of the relationship between stress-induced eating and the dampened chronic stress response network.

Conclusion

11. Research on the topic of food and mood has shown that the comfort foods many of us indulge in when we are experiencing stress or sadness are aptly named. These foods may provide temporary relief from negative emotions, but unfortunately this relief doesn't last. Increased consumption of comfort foods tends to leave us feeling down again a day or two later, which can drive us to consume yet more comfort foods, perpetuating a cycle of stress-induced emotional eating. Over time, chronic stress and emotional eating can lead to obesity, as our bodies' chronic stress response networks show decreased activity and we rely on comfort foods as medication for our stress. Many studies investigating food and mood have focused on women, as women are more likely to report increased comfort food consumption in response to distressing emotions. However, the findings of these studies have important implications for the health of both males and females, as obesity is a public health crisis in America.

12. The research on food and mood gives insight into the roles of both the body and mind in causing obesity. With a greater understanding of the roles of stress and other negative emotional states in causing the eating behaviors that can lead to obesity, we can help individuals cope with stressors in healthier ways. The bidirectional relationship between food and mood suggests that by avoiding overconsumption of comfort foods, we can break the perpetual cycle of stress-induced eating and end up healthier, both physically and emotionally. The next step should be to research the effectiveness of alternative coping mechanisms for stress and other negative emotions, such as mindfulness and exercise, and to develop ways to help individuals integrate these healthier coping mechanisms into their lives.

Reading Task

A review of the literature can:

- Set up a theoretical framework for your research;
- Establish the importance of the topic;
- Provide background information needed to understand the study;
- Show readers you are familiar with significant and/or up-to-date research relevant to the topic;
- Clarify important definitions/terminology;
- Establish your study as one link in a chain of research that is developing knowledge in your field.

Task one *Read the literature review above, and answer the following questions.*

1. What is the research focused on?

_____

2. What are the components of the literature review?

_____

3. How is the literature review organized?

_____

4. What are the topics and subtopics in the literature review?

_____

5. What studies are the evidence of a dampened chronic stress response network in response to stress-induced eating in rats and in humans?

_____

6. What conclusion has the author drawn from the literature review?

_____

Task two *Read the literature review again and find out the sentences or expressions which can be used in the corresponding part below.*

1. Give an introduction.

_____

2. Review the previous related studies.

_____

3. Make a comparison and contrast.

_____

4. State the limitation of previous research.

_____

5. Introduce further research.

_____

State the Methodology

This unit will explain in detail the over-all procedure you will follow in conducting your thesis. It includes detailed discussions of the design of the research, explanation of variables you will study, the description of participants/respondents from whom you shall collect your data, sampling procedures, description of research instruments you will use in collecting your data, steps you will follow in collecting data, and the methods and tools you will use to analyze your data. Sometimes, this is referred to as "Methods and Procedures".

When, after reading the methodology, one is able to explain what is going to be done, why it is going to be done, and how it is going to be done, then the methodology is well-developed and understandable.

Guidance and Structure of Writing the Methodology Section

The specific functions of the unit will therefore include the following aspects:
- A description and justification of the methodological approach
- A description and justification of the research design
- A description and justification of the specific methods employed for data collection
- A discussion of ways in which the validity and reliability of the data were achieved
- A description and justification of the data collection procedures
- A description and justification of the data analysis procedures

Although there is a built-in logic to the order in which the functions might be achieved, a logical argument can be achieved by describing and justifying the data collection processes before or after describing and justifying the design and methods employed in the study. The following are the parts needed to be included in the methodology section of an academic writing:

- **Participants or Subjects**: Who participate in the study? How did you choose the participants/subjects?
- **Materials or Instruments**: What are the features of the materials? What data collection instruments are used in the study?
- **Process or Procedure**: How to do the research? How the research method works?
- **Design and Analysis**: How to analyze the data (Statistical analysis/ Thematic analysis)? What are the instruments or software used to analyze the data? Why?

The following is the sample analysis of a thesis methodology chapter:

1) introduction of the chapter

1. In the U.S., nearly two-thirds of first-time community college students were required to take at least one developmental course in mathematics (Bahr, 2013). Despite the assistance and training they received in developmental courses, approximately 75% of those students did not successfully complete a mathematics course at the college level (Bahr, 2013; Fain, 2012). Consequently, about 50% of first-time community college students did not obtain a degree (Bahr, 2012). Research has shown that the higher the college completion rate the better the economy of a country (Davidovitch, Byalsky, Soen, & Sinuani-Stern, 2013). If the graduation rates continue to decline, the U.S. may lose its global competitiveness. One factor that led to low completion rates in developmental mathematics courses was the ineffectiveness of instructional strategies (Yuksel, 2010). It has been shown that — to be continued using a TLM strategy on students in the twenty-first century did not improve their motivation toward learning or academic achievement (Nafees, Farooq, Shaheen, & Akhtar, 2012). On the other hand, positive correlations between the incorporation of TBL strategies and student motivation and academic performance were documented in multiple disciplinary studies (Hsiung, 2012; Wong & Abbruzzese, 2011). Although TBL is becoming a favorable teaching strategy, the face-to-face lecture style remains the most common instructional methods at the college level (Carlson, 2013). In order to increase college completion rates for all students, improving student-learning experiences in developmental mathematics courses is becoming a growing national commitment (Cullinane & Treisman, 2010; Goldstein, Burke, Getz, Kennedy, 2011). Therefore, there was a need to measure the differences in individual student motivation and achievement in developmental mathematics courses	*Reason of choosing the methodology for the study*

as a result of incorporating TLM strategies as opposed to TBL strategy.

  2. The purpose of this quantitative, ex post facto study was to examine the differences in individual student motivation and achievement in developmental mathematics courses as a result of incorporating TBL strategy as opposed to TLM strategy. The study site was at a community college in San Antonio, Texas. According to a power analysis via G*Power (Faul et al., 2009), the study required at least 42 students, who enrolled in a three-hour credit developmental mathematics course in the community college. However, a total of 44 students, in which 21 students in the TLM group and 23 students in the TBL group, participated in this study. In order to recruit participants, the TSI (CORD, 2010; see Appendix A) was given to the professors in the participating institution. After identifying professors' teaching style to be either TLM or TBL, they distributed research materials along with a link to an online survey engine called SurveyMonkey® to students in their classes. The sample comprised of 21 students, who experienced a traditional face-to-face lecture style without the incorporation of social learning strategy, and 23 students, who received instruction that utilized a specific TBL strategy, called the SLO (see Appendix B). In order to measure student motivation, participants completed the pre and post CIS (Keller, 2010; see Appendix C), which assessed learners' motivation reaction to specific instructional environment. Each participant provided demographic information, as a part of the CIS, in order for information on sex, ethnicity, and age to be collected. Demographic information of students, including gender, ethnicity, and age was used as descriptive data. A comparison of student achievement was based on the differences of the pre and post ASQ (College Board, 2012; see Appendix D). A one-way MANOVA was used to measure the differences of incorporating TBL strategy on individual student motivation and achievement in college developmental mathematics courses.

Appropriateness of choosing the methodology

  Paragraph 1 explains why the methodological approach and research design have been chosen, namely, that they are the best suited to the investigation of the research.

  Paragraph 2 reveals that the quantitative, ex post facto method was chosen as the most appropriate for the research purpose.

2) Participants/Subjects

The student participants' ages ranged from 18 to 46 years (Mode = 19; M = 25.1, SD = 7.33). They were 37 in total, comprised of 15 males and 22 females. Almost all of the students were from Asia (84%). The nationality of the largest group was Japanese (40%) followed by Chinese (16%), Thai (8%), Korean (5%), Samoan (5%), and Vietnamese (5%); the other students (21%) were Israeli, Micronesian, Sri Lankan, Mexican, or French. The amount of time that the participants had studied English (Range = 0–18 years; M = 8.5 years, SD = 5.08) and had lived in English-speaking countries (Range =0.25–96 months; M = 17.5 months, SD = 21.57) varied widely. This study's participants are more heterogeneous than those of most of the previous ER motivation studies. The students are further described in Table 2.	*Location,*
As Table 2 shows, Peter's students at Institution Pre had studied English for a shorter time period than Ulrich's students at Institution Uni, a difference that might be expected given that Peter's students were at Institution Pre either as part of a university preparatory program (i.e., they had not yet begun to study at an English-speaking university) or as part of a study-abroad experience. Ulrich's students at Institution Uni had also lived longer in English-speaking countries, but were younger than Peter's students at Institution Pre. The age difference might be due to the fact that the students at Institution Uni were university students, who are typically of a similar age, as many of them enroll in university when they graduate from high school, whereas the student status of the students at Institution Pre was more diverse.	*size, context, characteristics*

Details of the characteristics of the participants that the author believes the reader should know are presented in "participation" and "subject" part, including background, gender ratio, age, learning background and learning context. There are two details that one might also consider, including, (1) providing a heading that includes the word "context" as well as "participants" or "subject" and (2) providing source justification for including the particular sample in the study. Concerning the latter, the reader might also find it useful to know why the particular proficiency level and context were chosen.

3) Materials or Instruments

Three instruments were used in this study in order to answer the research questions. Written permissions to use each instrument were obtained prior to recruiting participants and gathering data. The first instrument was the TSI (see Appendix A), which determined the teaching styles of mathematics teachers. The TSI had 12 questions with four statements in each question describing how a person teaches. Participants ranked the four statements in each question with scales from one (1) to four (4), with a "4" being the most descriptive statement that matched his or her response and the next most descriptive statement should receive a "3", then a "2" and finally a "1" being the least descriptive statement. Professors completed the 12-question TSI (CORD, 2010; see Appendix A), and each survey item was summed up as guided by the CORD in order to determine the teaching style. Based on the TSI scores, professors were classified by teaching style to be either TLM or TBL. The second instrument was the 16-question CIS (see Appendix C), which measured a student's reactions corresponding to classroom instruction (Keller, 2010). The CIS measured student motivation in four subscales: attention (4 items), which measured learners' interests in learning the course materials; relevance (4 items), which measured learners' level of connection between course materials and personal goals; confidence (4 items), which measured learners' level of self-assurances, and satisfaction (4 items), which measured learners' level of self-fulfillment of learning expectations (Keller, 1987). Each subscale in the CIS included four questions using a 5-point graded Likert scale, ranging from not true (1) to very true (5), were provided for each survey question (Karoulis, 2011). The response scale was ranged from one (1) to five (5) for each of the 16 statements. The last instrument was the ASQ (College Board, 2012; see Appendix D), which contained 20 multiple-choice mathematics questions corresponding to the curriculum standards guided by the SACS and the THECB. The College Board and Educational Testing Service established the ACCUPLACER testing program in 1985, and its main function was to determine if high school graduates were ready to take core courses at the college level (Elliot et al., 2012). The results and analyses from each of the three instruments were intended to be used to answer the research questions and validate the hypotheses.

Data collection instruments with justification

In the instrument section, the author introduces three methods employed in the data collection. Each of these methods were explained to give a clear picture of how the research data be collected. If we consider the whole of this section as one unit, sometimes, an author will also find it necessary to discuss the disadvantages of using a particular method, so this will typically be presented before or after the advantages. In the sample thesis, the author has explained how to implement particular method to solve each aspect of the research questions.

4) Process or Procedure

Participants were trained and tested individually. Trials began with the experimenter disorienting participants by blindfolding them and walking them randomly around the room, occasionally turning them slowly in circles, before stopping at one of four pseudo-randomized start positions located at the center of each wall. The blindfold was then removed, and participants were instructed to "find the correct corner" by approaching and pointing to their choice corner. During training trials, participants were allowed as many choices as needed to find the correct corner and received feedback after each choice; during testing trials no feedback was provided, and trials ended following a single choice.	*Steps of the process or procedure*

Process paragraphs are usually developed step-by-step in a chronological or logical sequence. And each step of the process/procedure is introduced by using sequencing markers.

5) Design and Analysis

Research Design This study follows a multiple-case study design (Yin, 2003). This method enables researchers to explore differences within and between cases, and it has its advantages and disadvantages. This type of study is considered robust and reliable (Baxter & Jack, 2008; Yin, 2003), but it can also be time-consuming and difficult to find appropriate cases for the methodology. Because comparisons will be drawn, it is crucial that the cases are chosen carefully so that the researcher can either "(a) predict similar results (a literal replication) or (b) predict contrasting results but for predictable reasons (a theoretical replication)" (Yin, 2003, p. 47). For this particular study, I expected contrasting results from the two cases considering the distinct teacher practices.	*Research design with justification*

Data Analysis

A one-way MANOVA, conducted using SPSS, was used to generate analyses in order to determine the differences in student motivation and achievement between the two learning groups, TLM versus TBL, after a four-week treatment period. A one-way MANOVA was chosen for the analytical method because there were two related dependent variables, and the test provided details for the differences in student motivation. One assumption of MANOVA was that there was no multicollinearity, meaning that the dependent variables were moderate correlated (Meyers, Gamst, & Guarino, 2006). Having a high or low multicollinearity could decrease liability (Grewal, Cote, & Baumgartner, 2004). One way to check multicollinearity was by using SPSS to perform a multiple linear regression (MLR). In order to generate a variance inflation factor (VIF) value, the dependent variables, motivation and achievement, were ran as the independent variables of the MLR. It was recommended that the VIF value to be in between 1 to 10 (Lin, 2008). Another assumption of MANOVA was the homogeneity of variances; therefore, the signification level reported by a Levene's test needed to be greater than 0.05 (Betz, 1987). According to a power analysis via G*Power (Faul et al., 2009), the study required a minimum of 42 students. When the number of participants reached the requirement of the power analysis, it was assumed that the samples were large enough so that the multivariate normality assumption holds. However, a test for skewness and kurtosis was conducted to determine normality. The other assumption was that the observations were independent, meaning that students were in the group of either TLM or TBL, so that no participant participated in both groups. A multivariate mode under the general linear model was to be the method to analyze the data.

Outline and justification of data analysis & processing method

In writing this section of a thesis, first decision needs to be made on the extent to which you are going to provide specific detail and illustrations from the thesis of analytical processes or whether this level of detail is going to be more helpful for the reader. Once the decision has been made, the focus should be on the outline of the key analytical and processing measures with the justification of the practice.

The Difference Between "Methodology" and "Method"

"Methodology" refers to the theoretical approach or framework that your study was situated in. As such, it will explain the extent to which you employed a quantitative, qualitative and/or multi-method approach. You will need to explain why you chose the approach that was used in your study. This will involve some reference back to the research questions/hypotheses and issues you investigated. Illustration of methodology needs to refer to the literature available on research methodology and on research already published in the area of investigation so that argument can be presented for the approach adopted for the study.

"Method" refers to the specific methods you employed in your data collection. Thus, you will need to describe the instruments and materials you used and explain why they were appropriate for the research questions/hypotheses you were investigating. The "methodology" will have informed the choice of "methods". In explaining why you chose particular methods, you will need to explain why they were chosen rather than other methods. Your justification will need to refer to the particular advantages that one method has over another. Inevitably, there will be some issues that you may not have been able to address, so these need to be acknowledged as limitations. Authors often refer to these in this chapter when talking about the scope or parameters of their study and refer to them again in the concluding chapter.

Qualitative Research vs. Quantitative Research

Research is the search for knowledge. It is an objective and systematic search for relevant information on a particular subject or topic. It aims at finding answers to questions by implementing scientific procedures. On the basis of nature of information, there are two standard ways of conducting a search: qualitative research and quantitative research.

Quantitative research, which originated in the natural sciences, was concerned with investigating things which could be observed and measured in some way. Later, in social science, questions arising from complex human interactions and the failure of statistically accurate findings and this gave rise to new research methods like qualitative observation and discovery, which attempts to investigate thoughts, values etc.

1. Features of Qualitative and Quantitative Research

What is qualitative research? Qualitative research is one that involves quality or kind, i.e., the research is to be made on human feelings, attitudes, values and thoughts of human beings on the basis of observations and interpretation. For instance: a marketing research regarding consumer's taste, preferences and choices, by analyzing their buying behavior is a qualitative research.

What is quantitative research? Quantitative research tries to quantify defined variables and establish cause and effect relationship by way of generating numerical data from a larger sample population. For instance: Research carried out to know the sales of various toothpaste brands in a quarter, by different companies of an industry, is a quantitative research.

What are the differences between qualitative and quantitative research? Actually, both are tools with the singular purpose to gather information data. It's better to look at them as tools like a hammer and a screwdriver. They aren't opposites. They're just tools that are used in different situations.

2. Differences between qualitative and quantitative research

- Qualitative research does not base their research on predetermined hypothesis, while quantitative research will have one or more hypotheses, or questions that they want to address.
- Qualitative research is usually exploratory, in that, it provides insights and understanding on the subject. Whereas, quantitative research is conclusive in nature, as it tests specific hypothesis and examines the relationship.
- Qualitative research deals with feelings, attitudes, opinions and thoughts of human beings, to determine the reasons behind those human behavior. On the other hand, quantitative research deals with hard facts and statistical data.
- Qualitative research uses purposive sampling, in which smaller sample sizes are selected to get in-depth understanding of the target population. As against, quantitative research uses random sampling, in which large and representative sample is selected in order to generalize results to the whole population.
- The data collected for qualitative research is verbal or narrative data, which can be analyzed through picture, objects and words. Conversely, in quantitative research, the data collected is numerical, which can be presented to charts, graphs and tables, etc.

3. Data Collection Method

Qualitative data is collected in textual form on the basis of observation and interaction with the participants, e.g. through participant observation, in-depth interviews, case study and focus groups. It is not converted into numerical form and is not statistically analyzed. The sample size is typically small, may be because the methods used such as in-depth interviews are time and labor intensive.

Quantitative data collection methods are much more structured than qualitative data collection methods. Quantitative data collection methods include various forms of experiments, surveys—online surveys, paper surveys, mobile surveys and kiosk surveys, interviews—face-to-face interviews, telephone interviews, and hybrid method. Strict procedure and statistical analysis permit researchers to discover complex causal relationships and to determine to what extent one variable influences another.

4. Mixed Method

Every method has its limitations and that the different approaches can be complementary. Being able to mix different approaches has the advantages of enabling triangulation. Triangulation, in statistics and the social sciences, is a research tactic that involves using two or more different ways to verify one result. For example, a qualitative study involving in-depth interviews or focus group discussions might serve to obtain information which will then be used to contribute towards the development of an experimental measure or attitude scale, the results of which will be analyzed statistically. Cohen and Manion (2000) define triangulation as an "attempt to map out, or explain more fully, the richness and complexity of human behavior by studying it from more than one standpoint".

In conclusion, a qualitative research develops a theory for a quantitative research to experiment on. Although the quantitative and qualitative research method have their weaknesses, they also possess their strengths. Therefore, both approaches are of value, in fact, they complement each other.

Vocabulary and Sentence Pattern for the Methodology Section

In order to complete the information, you need to write this section of your paper you now need to and use appropriate vocabulary for each part of Methodology.

1. Provide a general introduction and overview

all (of)	(the) tests	is/are available
both (of)	(the) samples	was/were carried out
each (of)	(the) trials	was/were conducted
many (of)	(the) experiments	was/were collected
most (of)	(the) equipment	was/were devised
the majority(of)	(the) chemicals	was/were generated
	(the) models	was/were modified
	(the) instruments	was/were obtained
	(the) materials	was/were performed
		was/were supplied
		was/were used as supplied
		was/were investigated

Here are some examples of how these are used:

- **The impact tests used in this work** were a modified version of...
- **All reactions** were performed in a 27 ml glass reactor...
- **All cell lines** were generated as previously described in...
- **In the majority of the tests**, buffers with a pH of 8 were used in order to...

- **Both experiments** were performed in a greenhouse so that...
- The substrate **was obtained from** the Mushroom Research Centre...
- SSCE glass structures **were used** in this study to perform...
- The cylindrical lens **was obtained from** Newport USA and is shown in Fig. 3.
- **The material investigated** was a standard aluminum alloy; all melts were modified with sodium.
- Topographical examination **was carried out** using a 3-D stylus instrument.
- **The experiments were conducted** at a temperature of 0.5℃.

2. Supply essential background information

opposite	facing	underneath
out of range (of)	within range (of)	on top (of)
parallel (to/with)	perpendicular (to)	adjacent (to)
on the right/left	to the right/left (to) converge	(to) intersect
(to) bisect	far side/end	border
near side	edge	in the front/back
downstream (of) boundary	upstream (of)	inner/outer
horizontal	margin	lateral
circular	vertical	conical
equidistant	rectangular	on each side
on either side	equally spaced	is located
is placed	is situated	is fastened (to)
is mounted (on)	is coupled (onto)	is fixed (to)
is aligned (with)	is connected (to)	is fitted (with)
extends	is surrounded (by)	is joined (to)
is attached to	is covered with/by	

Here are some examples of how these are used:

- Porosity was measured **at the near end and at the far end** of the polished surface.
- The compression axis **is aligned with** the rolling direction...
- The source light was polarized **horizontally**, and the sample beam can...
- ... be scanned **laterally**.
- The mirrors **are positioned near** the focal plane.
- Electrodes comprised a 4 mm diam disk of substrate material **embedded in** a Teflon disk of 15 mm diam.
- The intercooler **was mounted on top of** the engine...
- The concentration of barium decreases **towards the edge**...

- Similar loads were applied to **the front and side** of the box...
- A laminar ow element **was located downstream of** the test section of the wind tunnel...

3. Provide specific and precise details about materials and methods

was adapted	was eliminated	was operated
was added	was employed	was optimized
was adopted	was estimated	was plotted
was applied	was exposed	was positioned
was arranged	was extracted	was prepared
was assembled	was formulated	was quantified
was assumed	was generated	was recorded
was attached	was immersed	was regulated
was calculated	was inhibited	was restricted
was carried out	was incorporated	was retained
was characterized	was inserted	was sampled
was collected	was installed	was scored
was combined	was inverted	was selected
was computed	was isolated	was separated
was consolidated	was maintained	was simulated
was constructed	was maximized	was substituted
was controlled	was measured	was tracked
was created	was minimized	was transferred
was derived	was modified	was treated
was discarded	was normalized	was varied
was distributed	was obtained	was utilized

4. Justify choice made

by doing..., we were able to	provide a way of (+ -ing)
chosen for (+ noun)	selected on the basis of...
chosen to (+ infinitive)	so as to (+ infinitive)
for the purpose of (+ -ing or noun)	so/such that
for the sake of (+ -ing or noun)	so (+ -ing)
in an attempt to (+ infinitive)	thereby (+ -ing)
in order to (+ infinitive)	therefore
it was possible to (+ infinitive)	thus (+ -ing)
offer a means of (+ -ing)	to (+ infinitive)

one way to avoid... our aim was to (+ infinitive)	to take advantage of which/this allows/allowed etc. with the intention of (+ -ing)

Here are some examples of how these are used:

- **To validate** the results from the metroscale model, samples were collected from all groups.
- The method of false nearest neighbors was selected **in order to determine** the embedding dimension.
- **For the sake of** simplicity, only a single value was analyzed.
- **By partitioning** the array, all the multipaths could be identified.
- Zinc oxide was drawn into the laminate **with the intention of** enhancing delamination and cracks.
- **The advantage of** using three-dimensional analysis was that the out-of-plane stress field could be obtained.
- **Because** FITC was used for both probes, enumeration was carried out using two different slides.
- The LVDTs were unrestrained, **so allowing** the sample to move freely.
- The cylinder was constructed from steel, **which avoided** problems of water absorption.

Exercises

I. Reading

Task One *Read the following Methodology part and match each sentence with a short description of what the writer is doing.*

Changes in the chemistry of groundwater in the chalk of the London Basin *Methodology*	In this sentence, the writer:
1. The current investigation involved sampling and analyzing six sites to measure changes in groundwater chemistry.	1_____
2. The sites were selected from the London Basin area, which is located in the south-east of England and has been frequently used to interpret groundwater evolution.	2_____
3. A total of 18 samples was collected and then analyzed for the isotopes mentioned earlier.	3_____
4. Samples 1–9 were collected in thoroughly-rinsed 25ml brown glass bottles which were filled to the top and then sealed tightly to prevent contamination.	4_____

5. The filled bottles were shipped directly to two separate laboratories at Reading University, where they were analyzed using standard methods suitably miniaturized to handle small quantities of water.	5_____
6. Samples 10–18 were prepared in our laboratory using a revised version of the precipitation method established by the ISF Institute in Germany.	6_____ 7_____
7. This method obtains a precipitate through the addition of BaCl2.2H2O; the resulting precipitate can be washed and stored easily.	8_____
8. The samples were subsequently shipped to ISF for analysis by accelerator mass spectrometry (AMS).	9_____
9. All tubing used was stainless steel, and although two samples were at risk of CFC contamination as a result of brief contact with plastic, variation among samples was negligible.	

II. Writing: Write a Methodology section.

In the task, you will bring together and use all the information in this unit. You will write a Methodology section according to the model, using vocabulary and expressions you have learned.

Imagine that you are writing up a research project which has carried out the first-ever attempt to cook chicken. The title of the research paper in which you report the new process is: **An Approach to the Preparation of Chicken**. Imagine that until now, everyone ate it raw. The task is to write a recipe for cooking chicken as if it were the Materials/Methods section of a research paper. You should write approximately 250~400 words.

Present Results and Findings

The key purpose of this unit is to present the findings from your investigation to enable the reader to understand with ease how they address your research questions/hypotheses. In doing so, you will need, at times, to refer back to materials presented in your methodology and point the reader forward to what will be considered in the discussion of results chapter. As you present each finding, you will also need to think about whether or not an explanation should be given about what the finding means. Evidence (e.g., statistics, examples, tables or figures) from your data and analysis will feature frequently as you support your findings. In most cases, the results of your work can be given in graphs, tables, equations or images.

But there are many reasons for writing a Results section. In the first place, some of your results may be more interesting or significant than others, and it is difficult to communicate this in a table or graph. Also, it is essential to relate your results to the aim(s) of the research. Thirdly, in some cases you may want to offer background information to explain why a particular result occurred, or to compare your results with those of other researchers. In addition, your results may be problematic; perhaps some experiments were not fully successful, and you want to suggest possible reasons.

Guidance and Structure of Writing the Results Section

The structure of the Results section is most typically organized around the research questions/hypotheses. Sometimes, authors will present their results under thematic or topic headings that are relevant to the research questions/topics. Then again, some authors make use of thematic/topic headings within a research question/hypothesis structure. Having decided on your structure, you will need to decide on the order in which your specific findings will be presented. As you set about introducing each new finding, you will then need to consider what further information should be given to support that finding. And the Results section needs to contain, but not limited to, the following three elements: a location statement, important findings and brief comments of the findings, which can be illustrated by the following example:

1. Figure 1.1 shows the correlation between IQ and mortality risk in sample of nearly one million Swedish men.	*Location statement*
2. As can be seen, the risk of death (from any cause) in the 20 years following the IQ test was substantially higher for those with lower IQ scores.	*Main result*
3. The results suggested that the risk of death for the highest IQ category (group 9) is 1.0, the graph illustrates the comparative risk for the other groups.	*Specific result1*
4. The risk was over three times higher in the lowest IQ category (group1).	*Specific result2*
5. However, exactly what could explain the genetic link between IQ and mortality remains unclear and one possibility is that higher IQ contributes to optimal health behaviours, such as exercising and not smoking.	*Comments*

In Paragraph 1, the location statement indicated the graph (fig 1.1) is on which the result bases. Paragraph 2 suggests the main finding that there is a connection between the risk of death and IQ. However, this is rather vague, because what the connection exactly about is not explained in paragraph 2. The main result paragraph is supported by the details and data offered by paragraph 3 and 4, which are the most distinguishing data shown in fig 1.1. Finally, brief comments on the reasons of the phenomenon revealed by the data are suggested.

The following excerpt from an authentic academic thesis reveals in detail how to write the Results section:

A modelling approach to traffic management and CO exposure during peak hours
Results

1 Data obtained in previous studies using a fixed on-site monitor indicated that travel by car resulted in lower CO exposure than travel on foot. **2** According to Figo et al. (1999), the median exposure of car passengers was 11% lower than for those walking. **3** In our study, modelled emission rates were obtained using the Traffic Emission Model (TEM), a CO-exposure modelling framework developed by Ka. **4** Modelled results were compared with actual roadside CO concentrations measured hourly at a fixed monitor. **5** Figure 1 shows the results obtained using TEM. **6** As can be seen, during morning peak-time journeys the CO concentrations for car passengers were significantly lower than for pedestrians, which is consistent with results obtained in previous studies. **7** However, the modelled data were not consistent with these results for afternoon journeys. **8** Although the mean CO concentrations modelled by TEM for afternoon journeys on foot were in line with those of Figo et al., a striking difference was noted when each of the three peak hours was considered singly (Fig. 2). **9** It can be observed that during the first hour (H1) of the peak period, journeys on foot resulted in a considerably lower level of CO exposure. **10** Although levels for journeys on foot generally exceeded those modelled for car journeys during H2, during the last hour (H3) the levels for journeys on foot were again frequently far lower than for car journeys. **11** A quantitative analysis to determine modelling uncertainties was applied, based on the maximum deviation of the measured and calculated levels within the considered period. **12** Using this approach, the average uncertainty of the model prediction for this study slightly exceeds the 50% acceptability limit defined by Jiang. **13** Nevertheless, these results suggest that data obtained using TEM to simulate CO exposures may provide more sensitive information for assessing the impact of traffic management strategies than traditional on-site measurement.

In Sentences 1 and 2, the writer refers to the findings and conclusions obtained by other researchers. If you begin by describing individual results, the reader will need to build an overall scheme or pattern of your results by putting those individual results together. This is difficult for the reader to do; it is your job as a writer to arrange the information so that it is easy for a reader to process it. As with all subsections, therefore, it is more "reader-friendly" to start with some introductory material. When you start any new section or subsection in your work, the first sentence(s) should provide a smooth transition for the reader between the new (sub)section and the previous one.

In Sentences 3 and 4, the writer refers back to his/her own methodology and adds more information about it. You may decide to refer to or summarize your methodology in your opening sentences. One reason for doing this is to highlight the important aspects of the materials, equipment or methodology you used to obtain your results. Another reason is to remind your readers of the methodology. You remember it well, but your readers don't share that familiarity. Also, extended details of the methodology are often given here rather than in the previous section, which may have included only the basic framework of the method.

Background information is as common and as necessary here as elsewhere. In this case, information is provided about the instrument(s) or equipment used to obtain the results (a CO-exposure modelling framework developed by Ka3). Later, in the Results section you may need to provide more information in order to explain why a specific result occurred.

In Sentence 5, the writer invites the reader to look at a graph/figure/table, etc. What do you do when you are reading, and you come to a sentence like this? You stop reading and take a look at the figure; you try to understand it or interpret the data you see in it; then you return to the text and keep that interpretation in mind when you carry on reading. If the data in the figure is very clear and has only one possible interpretation, it doesn't matter when you invite your reader to look at it. In this case, the results are very clear and easily interpreted, and so it is safe to let the reader view them before you comment on them. However, the data in many figures, tables and photographs can be interpreted in more than one way, in which case you should comment on the results in that figure before you invite the reader to take a look. If not, the reader may interpret it differently from you.

In Sentence 6, the writer refers to specific results and compares them with those obtained in another study, using subjective, evaluative language. You need to show your reader how and where your results fit in with the existing research picture, so you need to compare your results with those in the literature.

As stated earlier, results do not speak for themselves. You do not have to use evaluative language in every case; sometimes results can be given objectively, either numerically or in non-evaluative language. However, if you simply describe what is in the figure or table, you have not added anything to what the reader can see for themselves. The comments you make on your results influence the way readers perceive them.

In Sentence 7, the writer offers a general statement about his/her results to begin a new paragraph.

In Sentence 8, the writer refers to specific results and compares them to those obtained in another study, using language that comments on the result(s). At some stage, you need to describe individual results in some detail, and select results which are important, typical, or especially interesting.

In Sentences 9 and 10 the writer selects specific results to describe in more detail, using language that comments on the results. Explanations can be given by providing background information to explain why a particular result occurred. Make sure that you understand the difference between the explanation of a result (why it occurred as it did), the evaluation of a result (what the numbers mean) and the implication of a result (what the result suggests or implies). At this stage your explanations should be limited to direct comments about your results; you will move on to broader explanations and implications in the Discussion/ Conclusion.

Some of your results are probably more significant than others. Choosing to describe a specific result in detail communicates to your reader that you consider that particular result to be significant, worth highlighting or emphasizing.

In Sentence11, the writer refers to the method used to analyze the results. The Methodology often only deals with the basic structure and components of the materials and methods. In such cases, most of the details are incorporated into the Results. This way of presenting information is quite common in science journals.

In Sentence 12, the writer mentions a problem in the results and uses quantity language (slightly) to minimize its significance. Don't ignore problems in your results unless you are certain that the problems are insignificant and invisible. If your results are incomplete or some of them don't "fit", you should mention this, minimize its importance if you can, and suggest possible reasons/offer a solution for the problem.

In Sentence 13, the writer makes a reference to the implications and applications of the work she/he has done. An examination of implications and applications is certainly one of the central areas of the Discussion, but most writers give some implication of what their results mean towards the end of the Results section.

Vocabulary and Sentence Pattern for the Result Section

1. Revisiting the research aim/existing research

as discussed previously,	it is known from the literature that...
as mentioned earlier/before,	it was predicted that...
as outlined in the introduction,	our aim/purpose/intention was to...
as reported,	since/because..., we investigated...
in order to..., we examined...	the aforementioned theory/aim/prediction, etc.
it is important to reiterate that...	we reasoned/predicted that...
to investigate..., we needed to...	

Here are some examples of how these are used:

- **Since** the angular alignment is critical, the effect of an error in orientation was **investigated experimentally.**
- **We reasoned that** an interaction in one network between proteins that are far apart in the other network may be a technology-specific artifact.
- **In earlier studies** attempts were made to establish degradation rate constants by undertaking ozonation experiments.
- **The main purpose of this work** was to test algorithm performance.
- **As mentioned previously, the aim of** the tests was to construct a continuous crack propagation history.
- **In this work, we sought to** establish a methodology for the synthesis of a benzoxazine

skeleton.

- **It was suggested in the Introduction** that the effective stress paths may be used to define local bounding surfaces.

2. General overview of results

in this section, we compare/evaluate/present...	on the whole
it is apparent that in all/most/the majority of cases, it is	generally speaking,
evident from the results that...	in general,
the overall response was...	in most/all cases,
the results are divided into two parts as follows: using	in the main,
the method described above, we obtained...	

Here are some examples of how these are used:

- **It is apparent that both** films exhibit typical mesoporous structures.
- **It is evident** that these results are in good agreement with their FE counterparts.
- **In general**, coefficients for months close to the mean flowering data were negative.
- Our confidence scores have an **overall** strong concordance with previous predictions.
- **On the whole**, the strains and deflections recorded from the FE model follow similar patterns to those recorded from the vacuum rig tests.
- Levels of weight loss were similar **in all cases**.

3. Invitation to view results

Figure 1:	as detailed in Fig.1
contains	as evident from/in the figure
corresponds (to)	as illustrated by Fig. 1
demonstrates	as indicated in. Fig.1
displays	as listed in Fig.1
gives	as we can see from/in Fig.1...
illustrates	can be identified from/in Fig.1
lists	can be observed in Fig. 1
plots	comparing Figs. 1 and 4 shows that...
presents	data in Fig. 1 suggests that...
provides	displayed in Fig. 1
reports	evidence for this is in Fig. 1
represents	inspection of Fig. 1 indicates...
reveals	is/are represented (etc.) in
shows	is/are visible in Fig. 1
summarizes	in Fig. 1 we compare/present etc....

Here are some examples of how these are used:

- The stress data in Fig. 18 **indicates** a more reasonable relationship.
- Figure 3 **illustrates** the findings of the spatial time activity modelling.
- The overall volume changes are **reported** in Fig. 6(d).
- Similar results were found after loading GzmA into the cells (**data not shown**).
- Typical cyclic voltammograms **can be seen in Fig. 1**.
- **Comparing Figs. 1 and 4** shows that volumetric strains developed after pore pressure had dissipated.
- The rate constants shown in Table 1 **demonstrate that** the reactivity is much greater at neutral pH.
- The results **are summarized** in Table 4.

4. Specific/key results in detail

Objective description

accelerate(d)	is/are/was/were constant	match(ed)
all change(d)	is/are/was/were different	none
decline(d)	is/are/was/were equal	occur(red)
decrease(d)	is/are/was/were found	peak(ed)
delay(ed)	is/are/was/were higher	precede(d)
drop(ped)	is/are/was/were highest	produce(d)
exist(ed)	is/are/was/were identical	reduce(d)
expand(ed)	is/are/was/were lower	remain(ed) constant
fall/fell	is/are/was/were present	remained the same
find/found	is/are/was/were unchanged	rise/rose
increase(d)	is/are/was/were uniform	vary/varied

Here are some examples of how these are used:

- There was a **lower** proportion of large particles present at lower pH.
- As can be seen in Fig. 8, there were **different** horizontal and vertical directional pseudofunctions.
- As can be seen, in the second trial the level of switching among uninformed travelers **was unchanged**.
- This kind of delamination **did not occur** anywhere else.
- The CTOA **dropped** from its initial high value to a constant angle of 40.
- It eventually **levelled off** at a terminal velocity of 300 m/s.

Subjective description

abundant(ly)	imperceptible(ibly)	remarkable(ably)
acceptable(ably)	in particular	resembling satisfactory
adequate(ly)	inadequate(ly)	scarce(ly)
appreciable(ably)	interesting(ly)	severe(ly)
appropriate(ly)	it appears that	similar(ly)
brief(ly)	main(ly)	smooth(ly)
comparable(ably)	marked(ly)	steep(ly)
considerable(ably)	measurable(ably)	striking(ly)
consistent(ly)	mild(ly)	substantial(ly)
dominant(ly)	minimal(ly)	sufficient(ly)
dramatic(ally)	noticeable(ably)	suitable(ably)
equivalent(ly)	obvious(ly)	the majority of
essential(ly)	overwhelming(ly)	too + adjective
excessive(ly)		unexpected(ly)

Here are some examples of how these are used:

- In **the majority of** cases, SEM analysis revealed a **considerably** higher percentage of fine material.
- As can be seen, the higher injection rate gave **satisfactory** results from all three methods.
- **Similar** behavior was observed in all cases, with no **sudden** changes.
- It can be seen in Fig. 5 that the Kalman filter gives an **excellent** estimate of the heat released.
- The effect on the relative performance was **dramatic**.
- A **striking** illustration of this can be seen in Fig. 5.
- Comparing Figs. 4 and 5, it is obvious that a **significant** improvement was obtained in **the majority of** cases.
- It can be observed from Fig. 5 that the patterns are **essentially** the same in both cases.
- Figure 1 shows a **fairly** consistent material.
- It can be observed from Fig. 2 that there was **only** a **very small** enhancement when H_2O_2 was present.

5. Possible implications of results

apparently	it is logical that
could be due to	it is thought/believed that
could be explained by	it seems that

could account for	it seems plausible (etc.) that likely
could be attributed to	may/might
could be interpreted as	means that
could be seen as	perhaps
evidently	possibly/possibility
imply/implies that	potentially
indicate/indicating that	presumably
in some circumstances	provide compelling evidence
is owing to	suggest(ing) that
is/are associated with	support the idea that
is/are linked to	tend to
is/are related to	tendency
it could be concluded that...	unlikely
it could be inferred that	there is evidence for
it could be assumed that	we could infer that
it is conceivable that	we have confidence that
it is evident that	would seem to suggest/indicate

Here are some examples of how these are used:

- **This suggests that** silicon is intrinsically involved in the precipitation mechanism.
- These curves **indicate that** the effective breadth is a minimum at the point of application of the load.
- Empirically, **it seems that** alignment is most sensitive to rotation in depth.
- Only the autumn crocus produced a positive response, **suggesting that** other species would flower earlier under climate warming.
- **It could be inferred** therefore that these **may have** reacted with ozone to form organic acids, such as formic acid.
- **It indicates that** no significant crystalline transformations occurred during sintering.
- **It is therefore speculated that** at pH 7.5 a major part of the reaction was via hydroxyl radical attack.
- **It is apparent that** this type of controller **may be** more sensitive to plant/model mismatch than was assumed in simulation studies.
- Results **seem to indicate that** this causes the behavior to become extremely volatile.
- **It is evident that** the ψ at midspan increases with the increasing.

Exercises

I. Reading: After completing a study or an experiment, the author will present a collection of data and observation which is produced in the Results section and provide explanations for these findings. Read the Results part of the following thesis and finish the following writing tasks.

The introduction, methods, results, and discussion (IMRAD) structure: a fifty–year survey

Luciana B. Sollaci, MS, Library Director1 and Mauricio G. Pereira[2]

RESULTS

The frequency of articles written using the IMRAD structure increased over time. In 1935, no IMRAD article could be found. In 1950, the proportion of articles presented in this modern form surpassed 10% in all journals. Thereafter, a pronounced increase can be observed until the 1970s, when it reached over 80%. During the first 20 years, from 1935 to 1955, the pace of IMRAD increments was slow, from none to 20%. However, during the following 20 years, 1955 to 1975, the frequency of these articles more than quadrupled (Figure 1).

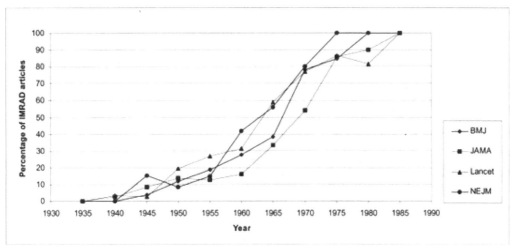

Figure 1

Proportion of introduction, methods, results, and discussion (IMRAD) adoption in articles published in the British Medical Journal, JAMA, The Lancet, and the New England Journal of Medicine, 1935–1985 (n = 1,297)

All four journals presented a similar trend: the New England Journal of Medicine fully adopted the structure in 1975, followed by the British Medical Journal in 1980, and JAMA and The Lancet in 1985.

Regarding the non-IMRAD articles, the evolution and variations of text organization for all journals can be delineated. In the British Medical Journal and The Lancet, articles that used non-IMRAD headings prevailed from 1935 to 1945. A shift to articles that partially adopted the IMRAD structure occurred from 1950 to 1960. From 1965 and beyond, the full structure tends to predominate. Until 1960, texts with different headings and partial IMRAD headings shared the lead in JAMA. From 1965 onward, the complete format is the most used. The New England Journal of Medicine had a slightly different pattern. Until 1955, continuous text, non-IMRAD headings, and case reports predominated. After 1960, the IMRAD structure takes the lead.

As an example, Figure 2 shows the text organization in the British Medical Journal from 1935 to 1985. The ascending curve represents the IMRAD articles. It is the same as shown in Figure 1, and the descending curves represent all other forms of text organization. A similar tendency was observed for The Lancet, JAMA, and the New England Journal of Medicine.

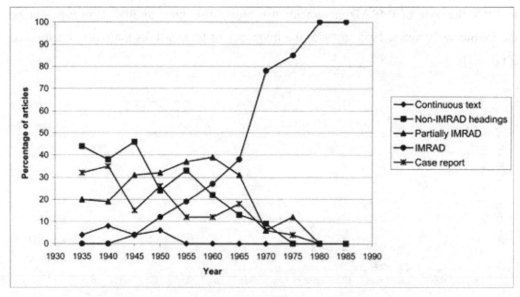

Figure 2

Text organization of published articles in the British Medical Journal from 1935 to 1985 (n = 341)

One interesting finding is that during the initial period of our study, the order of the IMRAD headings did not follow today's convention; results could be presented before methods or discussion before results, and, although a few articles followed the IMRAD structure in the 1940s, they were not the same as articles written with the IMRAD structure in the 1980s. Information, which today is highly standardized in one section, would be absent, repeated, or dispersed among sections in earlier articles.

Task one *Read the Results section and find out the information required below.*

1. Find out the statement that locates the figure(s) where the results can be found.

1). _____

2). _____

2. Find out the statements that present the most important findings.

_____

_____

3. Find out the author's brief comment.

_____

_____

4. What does the Results section include?

_____

_____

Task two *Actually, it would be difficult to come to definite conclusions just based on the very small amount of evidence that you have. So, it is very common in academic writing to be careful about any claims we make when discussing the results of our studies. Please find the tentative language in the discussion section.*

_____

_____

_____

II. Writing: Write a Result section.

Imagine that you have just completed a research project which has been investigating a possible link between UFO (Unidentified Flying Object) sightings and earthquake prediction. The task in this exercise is to evaluate your data and findings as if you were writing the Results section of a research paper. Using Table 1 below, write the Results section of this paper. The title of your research paper is **The earthquake lights theory: an analysis of earthquake—related UFO sightings**. You should write approximately 300~400 words. You can make up facts and references for this exercise.

Table: UFO sightings within 300km of epicenter

Country	UFO sightings for 7 days prior to earthquake	Earthquake magnitude	Average weekly UFO sightings	Description of UFO
Russia	44	3.2	11	*Green ball of light*
India	15	4.4	18	*Fast–moving disc*
Australia	120	6.0	30	*White ashes of light*
USA	275	5.6	75	*Clusters of high–speed light*
Canada	42	2.6	6	*Blue–green egg–shaped object*

Compose Discussion/Conclusion

The Discussion section of your dissertation is the chapter where you can speak truly from your own voice and share with your readers your thoughts, interpretations of your data analysis and supported opinions on the topic you have researched. For many scholars it is the most liberating chapter to write. If the Introduction section moves from a general, broad focus to the narrower "report" section of the paper, the Discussion/Conclusion moves away from that narrow section to a wider, more general focus. The Discussion looks back at the points made in the Introduction on the basis of the information in the central report section.

Guidance and Structure of Writing the Discussion/Conclusion Section

When you have analyzed your results, you are much more proficient than when you started your project, but you now have to establish what can be concluded from these results. This is where you can advance from information to knowledge, where you might be able to establish new theories or new ways of looking at things. This is the task of the discussion chapter. This is probably the part of your thesis where it is most important that you show your ability as a critical thinker. How can you design a structure for the Discussion that will enable you to get logically to your conclusions when you don't know what they are? The key to writing the Discussion is for you to bring these unconscious conclusions to the conscious realm and commit them to screen or paper. Your rational brain can then sort them out and do its best to make sense of them. And the Discussion section needs to have the following necessary elements:

- Synthesize your data/findings.
- State the implications of your findings in terms of theoretical, policy and practical implications.

- State the recommendations of your research based on your data findings.
- Clearly state and write out the limitations of your research.
- Provide suggestions for future research based on your findings.

Now, let's see how these elements are realized in the following example of a thesis discussion section:

Discussion

1 Prior work has documented the effectiveness of psychosocial intervention in improving quality of life (QoL) and reducing stress in patients suffering from various disorders; Epstein,18 for example, reports that orthopedic patients participating in a two-week multimedia intervention program improved across several QoL indices, including interpersonal conflict and mental health. 2 However, these studies have either been short-term studies or have not focused on patients whose disorder was stress related. 3 In this study we tested the extent to which an extended three-month stress management program improved QoL among a group of patients being treated for stress-related skin disorders such as eczema. 4 We found that in virtually all cases, participation in our three-month stress management program was associated with substantial increases in the skills needed to improve QoL.

5 These findings extend those of Kaliom, confirming that a longer, more intensive period of stress-management training tends to produce more effective skills than when those skills are input over a shorter period via information transfer media such as leaflets and presentations (Kaliom et al., 2003). 6 In addition, the improvements noted in our study were unrelated to age, gender or ethnic background. 7 The study therefore indicates that the benefits gained from stress-management intervention may address QoL needs across a wide range of patients.

8 Most notably, this is the first study to our knowledge to investigate the effectiveness of extended psychosocial intervention in patients whose disorder is itself thought to be stress-related. 9 Our results provide compelling evidence for long-term involvement with such patients and suggest that this approach appears to be effective in counteracting stress that may exacerbate the disorder.

10 However, some limitations are worth noting. 11 Although our hypotheses were supported statistically, the sample was not reassessed once the program was over. 12 Future work should therefore include follow-up work designed to evaluate whether the skills are retained in the long term and also whether they continue to be used to improve QoL.

In Sentence 1, the writer revisits previous research. By offering an overview of the previous section, the writer refers back to something from the previous sections to link it with the new one. Many Discussions/Conclusions begin by referring back to something from

the previous sections. This can consist of:
- revisiting the Introduction to restate the aims of the paper, important background factual information, the original prediction/theory/assumption or the problem the study was designed to solve.
- revisiting the Methodology for a reminder of the rationale for the procedures followed or a summary of the procedures themselves.
- revisiting the Results for a summary of the results obtained by others or by the author.

In Sentence 2, the writer revisits the Introduction to recall specific weakness in the methodology used in previous studies. Since the contribution of this paper is the difference between the methodology in previous research and that used here, the writer first revisits the gap/problem in the Introduction to recall the weaknesses in previous methodology which have been addressed in the present work, and then moves on to the specific differences between the methodology in the present work and that of previous work.

In Sentence 3, the writer revisits the methodology used in this study. Using the same language as in the Methodology will help the reader to remember the principles of your method, and it is common to recall significant features of your method here.

In Sentence 4, the writer revisits and summarizes the results. One of the central functions of the Discussion is to go beyond the results, to lead the reader away from a direct and narrow focus on your results towards the conclusions and broader implications or generalizations that can be drawn from those results. Summarizing the results provides an appropriate starting point for that process.

In Sentence 5, the writer shows where and how the present work fits into the research "map" of this field. In the short literature review in the Introduction, you gave your reader a picture of the current state of research in your field. You now need to show your readers how and where your study fits into that picture and in what way it changes or affects the research "map" in this area. In the Discussion, it is your responsibility to make the relationship between your study and other work explicit.

In Sentence 6, the writer recalls an aspect of the results that represents a positive achievement or contribution of this work. A very important feature of the Discussion is a clear focus on the achievement or contribution of your work. Specify the nature of your achievements, using positive language that clearly presents the benefits or advantages. Although you are aware of what is good about the work you have done and the results you have obtained, if you do not state it explicitly, the reader may not realize the value of your achievement.

In Sentence 7, the writer focuses on the meaning and implications of the achieve-

ments in this work. In the Discussion it is your responsibility to suggest why results occurred as they did and offer an explanation of the mechanisms behind your findings and observations. These suggestions, explanations and implications are refined, developed and discussed here. One important difference between result and discussion is that the aim of research is not simply to obtain and describe results; it is to make sense of those results in the context of existing knowledge and to say something sensible and useful about their implications. Saying what your results are is the central function of the Results section; talking about what they mean is the central function of the Discussion.

If you look at the way implications are stated in the Discussion, you will see recognize a wide use of tentative language used in this section. "It seems that/suggests that/indicates that" are common here, and there is a strong reliance on modal verbs such as may and could. This is because science research never reaches an endpoint where everything is known about a particular topic; the next piece of research will refine and develop the preceding one, and so on. As a result, most science writers are careful not to make unqualified generalizations, and as you can see from the words in this example, this writer is no exception.

In Sentence 8, the writer notes that one of the achievements or contributions of this work is its novelty. One of the significant achievements of this work is precisely the fact that a study of this type has not been done before. It is difficult to be absolutely sure that no-one has ever done a particular type of study until now, so before you make such a statement you should check as thoroughly as possible. As we can see in Sentence 8, even after every effort has been made, the writer nevertheless includes the phrase to our knowledge in case a study has been overlooked accidentally.

In Sentence 9, the writer refines the implications of the results, including possible applications. Developing the implications of your work includes looking at ways in which your results might be implemented or lead to applications in the future. In this case, the results imply that long-term involvement should be an aspect of future treatment.

In Sentences 10 and 11, the writer describes the limitations which should direct future research. The reason for mentioning the limitations of your study in the Discussion is to point out a direction for future work. You should therefore examine your study for limitations which can be addressed in future work, rather than limitations which are unlikely to be solved in the near future.

In Sentence 12, the writer suggests a specific area to be addressed in future work. One paper will not answer all possible questions in your research area, so when you are writing the Discussion, you should keep the broader picture in mind. Where should the research go next? The best studies open up directions for research. Inviting the research community to follow your work in a specific way has many functions.

Vocabulary and Sentence Pattern for the Discussion Section

1. Revisiting and Summarizing the Previous Section

When you revisit the previous sections, don't change the words in the sentences unnecessarily; your aim is to create an "echo" that will remind the reader of what you said before, so repeating the same words and phrases is advantageous.

2. Relationship to Existing Research

This is/Our study/method/result/approach is analogous to comparable to compatible with consistent with identical (to) in contradiction to in contrast to in good agreement (with) in line with significantly different (to/from) the first of its kind similar (to) unlike	This is/Our study broadens challenges compares well (with) confirms contradicts corresponds to differs (from) extends goes against lends support to provides insight into refutes supports verify

Here are some examples of how these are used:

- **To the knowledge of the authors,** the data in Figs. 4–6 is the **first of its kind**.
- The results of this simulation therefore **challenge** Laskay's assumption that percentage porosity increases with increasing Mg levels.
- The GMD method provides results that **are comparable to** existing clay hydration processes.
- **Similar** films on gold nanoparticles have also been found to be liquid-like.
- Using this multi-grid solver, load information is propagated **faster** through the mesh.
- Our results are **in general agreement with** previous morphometric and DNA incorporation studies in the rat [2.6].
- Our current findings **expand** prior work.
- The system described in this paper is **far less** sensitive to vibration or mechanical path

changes than previous systems.
- **Unlike** McGowan, we did not identify 9-cis RA in the mouse lung.

3. Achievement/Contribution

Useful adjectives:	Useful verbs:
accurate	assist
appropriate	compare well with
attractive	confirm
beneficial	enhance
comprehensive	ensure
convincing	facilitate
cost-effective	improve
feasible	offer an understanding of
flexible	outperform
productive	provide a framework
stable	remove the need for
straightforward	represent a new approach to
undeniable	reveal
valid	rule out

Here are some examples of how these are used:

- The presence of such high levels is a **novel** finding.
- We identify **dramatically** different profiles in adult lungs.
- Our results **provide compelling evidence** that this facilitated infection.
- These preliminary results demonstrate the **feasibility** of using RI detectors.
- Our data **rules out** the possibility that this behavior was a result of neurological abnormality.
- The system presented here is a **cost–effective** detection protocol.
- A **straightforward** analysis procedure was presented which **enables** the **accurate** prediction of column behavior.

4. Limitations/Current and Future Research

a/the need for	possible direction
at present	promising
encouraging	recommend
fruitful	remain to be (identified)

further investigations	research opportunities
further work is needed	should be explored
further work is planned	should be replicated
future work/studies should	should be validated
future work/studies will	should be verified
in future, care should be taken	starting point
in future, it is advised that...	the next stage
holds promise	urgent
it would be beneficial/useful	worthwhile

Here are some examples of how these are used:

- Our results are **encouraging** and **should be validated** in a larger group of women.
- However, the neural mechanisms of these effects **remain to be** determined.
- This finding is **promising** and **should be explored** with other eukaryotes.
- **Future work should** focus on the efficacy of ligands synthesized in ...
- An important question for **future studies** is to determine the antidepressant effects of such drugs.

5. Application/Implementation

eventually	apply
in future	have potential
soon	implement
possible	lead to
	produce
	use
	utilize

Here are some examples of how these are used:

- Our technique **can be applied to** a wide range of simulation applications.
- The PARSEX reactor therefore could be **used** for the realistic testing of a wide range of control algorithms.
- It **should be possible**, therefore, to integrate the HOE onto a microchip.
- This approach **has potential** in areas such as fluid density measurement.
- The solution method **could be applied** without difficulty to irregularly-shaped slabs.
- Our results mean that in dipping reservoirs, compositional gradients can now **be produced** very quickly.
- This could **eventually lead to** the identification of novel biomarkers.

Tentativeness in the Writing of the Discussion Section

It is very common in academic writing to be careful about any claims we make when discussing the results of our studies. This is because it would be difficult to come to definite conclusions based on the very small amount of evidence that you have. In other words, it is necessary to make decisions about your stance on a particular subject, or the strength of the claims you are making to avoid being too dogmatic.

Tentative language is particularly useful in the Results and Discussion sections. In these sections you are writing about the reasons, interpretations and implications of your results and you often need to communicate that something is a possible reason, or an obvious interpretation or a probable implication. Here is a typical example from a Discussion section:

*It is **theoretically true that** the number of genes affected in a GM plant most likely **will be far**, far smaller than in conventional breeding techniques. However, opponents maintain that because the wholesale swapping or alteration of entire packages of genes is a natural process that has been happening in plants for half a billion years, **it tends to** produce few scary surprises today. Changing a single gene, on the other hand, **might** turn out to be a more subversive action, with unexpected ripple effects, including the production of new proteins that **might be** toxins or allergens.*

There are tentative expressions commonly used in the Discussion section:

Verbs
aim, appear, assume, can, could, estimate, indicate, infer, intend, may, might, presume, propose, seem, seen as, should, speculate, suggest, suppose, tend to

e.g. ***It appears that*** *the increase in crime is a result of high unemployment.*

e.g. *Industrialisation **tends to** be viewed as a better way of life.*

Nouns
appearance, indication, inference, likelihood, possibility, probability, suggestion, tendency, to our knowledge

e.g. ***There is a likelihood that*** *crime will increase in the next ten years.*

Adverbs
about, apparently, arguably, fairly, in general, largely, likely, more or less, mostly, often, perhaps, possibly, presumably, probably, quite, rather, somewhat, unlikely, usually

e.g. *It is **unlikely** that a reduced speed limit will result in fewer injuries.*

Exercises

I. Rewrite these sentences by using tentative language.

1. Playing violent video games causes more aggression, bullying, and fighting.

2. Mars is the focus of much scientific study and the foremost planet for human colonization.

3. News reports can never be trusted because of media bias, journalist interpretation and agenda setting.

4. Most people think that climate change is caused by human activities.

II. Read the Discussion and Conclusion part of a thesis and finish the following writing tasks.

In a strange and uncharted land: ESP teachers' strategies for dealing with unpredicted problems in subject knowledge during class

HuiDan Wu, Richard G. Badger

6. Findings and discussion

1. We have presented five episodes which illustrate how the three ESP teachers in our research context coped with ISKD situations together with their own comments on their behavior in two general patterns. Tables 2 and 3 present what we see as the key findings.

When teachers in our data had to deal with an unplanned subject knowledge problem, they either avoided the question or took a risk. None of the teachers chose to admit ignorance because of the loss of face this would involve. This may be a feature of our particular context, but we would not be surprised to see a similar dislike for admitting ignorance in other contexts. In addition, the structured interviews showed a strong preference for avoidance of risk taking in this context.

6.1. Factors influencing the response to ISKDs

2. The study has cast some light on the "complex networks of knowledge, thoughts and beliefs" (Borg, 2003, p. 81) that inform teachers' decisions. In broad terms, the teachers were concerned to maintain the smooth flow of the class, though this was closely related to the need to maintain face. There were at least three aspects of the ISKDs which appeared to affect the choice of strategy. The first was whether the ISKD arose from language in the materials or the language the teacher used, with language in the materials creating a greater risk of loss of face. It was relatively easy for Sophia in ISKD 1 to avoid explaining where the "engine room" was because this was not raised in the materials. In contrast, Jenny in ISKD 2 and ISKD 3 was at greater risk of losing face over "dry-docked" and "stores" because the explanation of these items was more central to the teaching materials.

3. The second aspect was who identified the ISKD. Where the ISKD was not explicitly mentioned by anyone, as in ISKD 1, there was little or no risk of loss of face. If someone identified the ISKD, there was less risk of loss of face if this was the teacher, as in ISKD 5 where Sophia asked the students about the "Service Department". In contrast, when a student asked a question, as in ISKD 4, the risk is greater. A linked factor here was that, where the teacher identified the problem, this was likely to mean she would have more time to identify a way of handling the ISKD effectively.

4. The third aspect related to the teacher's role as expert and how much credit the teacher had earned. In four of the five instances, the teacher had provided a translation of the problematic term and this contributed to the relatively smooth flow of the lesson. The one exception in ISKD 4 created a much more difficult problem for Anna and led to her adopting the risk-taking tactic of word-by-word translation, which she seems to have found less than perfect. The frequency of translation in our data also reflected the importance of this technique in this context but the fact that the teachers did not regard translation as a complete response to explaining what items meant suggested that the conceptualization of subject knowledge by the teachers went beyond what we might term purely linguistic knowledge.

5. There was some variation in how the teachers conceptualized the relationship between what they and the subject specialists might be expected to know, but broadly, the teachers felt they should have more than linguistic knowledge.

6.2. The influence of context

6. One of the striking features of the data was the similarity between the ways the different teachers behaved. This was apparent in the fact they all followed their lesson plans very closely and felt that divergences from the lesson plan indicated something had gone wrong. This may have been a result of being observed but we would argue that this reflects a more permanent feature of this educational context and may be related to the status of teachers in the Confucian tradition, though it is consistent with the desire of teachers outside the Confucian tradition for lessons with a smooth flow of activities (Borg, 2006). The teachers were clearly anxious to save face by not revealing their ignorance, though not particularly to be seen as dominating the class.

7. Conclusion

7. The study reported here was carried out on a relatively small scale and it would not be fair to make any broad generalizations based on what we found. We would like to suggest, however, that it may have implications for teacher development within the context in which the research was carried out and, possibly, more widely. Despite the influence of the local educational culture, teacher cognitions and practices do vary. The two risk-taking episodes indicate that there is, at least, the possibility for teachers to develop new ways of dealing with ISKDS that are culturally appropriate and pedagogically sound. Our research suggests four specific teacher cognitions that might be more widely disseminated:

1. Most (and probably all) teachers face ISKD situations.

2. The occurrence of an ISKD situation does not necessarily reflect poorly on the teacher.

3. There are many ways of dealing with ISKD.

4. ESP teachers, subject specialist teachers and students are all potential sources of information about the subject specialism and its language.

8. The changes in cognition could come about as part of pre- or in-service courses but also through peer observation and, perhaps the most practicable approach in this context, the study of transcripts of classroom interaction made available, for example, through research such as this. We hope that this study has provided some information about a relatively unexplored aspect of ESP teaching and created some impetus for future studies.

Task One *Read the Results section and find out the information required below.*

1. Find out the paragraph(s) that revisit the Methodology and the Results part.

_____
_____

2. Find out the paragraph(s) that present the most important findings.

_____
_____

3. Find out the statement(s) that indicate the limitation of the study.

_____
_____

4. Find out the statement(s) that predict the future research scope.

_____
_____

Task Two *Actually, it would be difficult to come to definite conclusions just based on the very small amount of evidence that you have. So, it is very common in academic writing to be careful about any claims we make when discussing the results of our studies. Please find the tentative language in paragraph 7.*

_____
_____

III. Write a Discussion/Conclusion.

Imagine that you and your team have designed a machine which can remove chewing gum from floors and pavements by treating the gum chemically to transform it into powder and then using vacuum suction to remove it. In the Methodology you described the design and construction of the machine. You compared your CGRM, GumGone, to two existing machines, Gumsucker and Vacu-Gum. You then gave details of a set of trials which you conducted to test the efficiency of the new CGRM and a further set of trials which showed the effect of gum removal on the floor surface.

In the Results section, you showed results of these trials. You compared the performance of GumGone with Gumsucker and Vacu-Gum. Your results were very good, and they can be seen in the tables below. Now write the Discussion/Conclusion.

Table 1: Gum removal as a percentage of total sample

	Gumsucker	Vacu-gum	GumGone
Wooden floor	77	73	80
Stone floor	78	78	82
Carpeted floor	56	44	79

Table 2: Floor damage/staining

	Gumsucker	Vacu-gum	GumGone
Wooden floor	Minimal	Minimal	None
Stone floor	Significant	Some	None
Carpeted floor	Significant	Significant	Minimal

Write the Abstract

An abstract is a brief summary of your entire dissertation. That is why this unit is kept until the very end. You need to have all of the information from the background of your study to the recommendations in order to write your abstract well. The challenge will be the maximum number of words allowed for the abstract. Universities may limit the number of words used in an abstract from 350 words to 500 words for dissertations. Academic journals and conferences will also impose their own word limit which may be as low as 100~200 words, so that you need to be aware of this guideline as well. Good abstract writing is necessary for both your dissertation, as well as future scholarly articles that you will write for submission to academic journals or conferences. A reader should be able to quickly read the abstract and be able to understand all of the necessary details of your research. Keeping the abstract short, tight and concise is, therefore, vital.

Guidance and Structure of Writing the Abstract

The Abstract was printed at the top of a research article and its function was mainly to encourage the reader to continue reading the article and to facilitate that reading by providing a brief preview. It should make sense as a standalone, self-contained description of the research article, and readers should be able to understand the key points and results of the research even if they never see the whole article. The Abstract is a representation of the research article. A reader should be able to quickly read the abstract and be able to understand all of the necessary details of the research. The most commonly used format for abstract writing has five parts:

(1) Background/Introduction

(2) Research Design/Research Methodology

(3) Findings/Results

(4) Recommendations/Implication/Significance

(5) Conclusion

Each part serves a specific purpose and will be elaborated for you below.

1. Background/ Introduction

The background information that is found at the start of the Abstract is usually derived from the first sentences of the Introduction.

Give a concise summary of the background of the research. Leave out unnecessary and flowery language and focus on the essence of the background. If you feel that a lot of background is necessary to understand the Abstract itself, combine the relevant points and summarize them in as few words as possible. The focus of an Abstract is more likely to be on the methodology or the results, so limit background information to one or two sentences.

In order to illustrate this point, let us say that your research is on crimes, such as rape and sexual harassment allegedly caused by the way women are dressed and portrayed in the media. The purpose of your research is to lower sex crimes committed against women through policy advocacy for media change and social education. You could then write your Background/Introduction as:

The perpetration of sexual crime is linked to gendered portrayals of women's attire in the media. However, detractors of this position believe that media portrayals are not responsible for the perpetration of such crimes. This research study questions the validity of these gendered portrayals from the perspective of feminism.

You can reduce the number of words by combining the background information and the aim or the research questions, so that the sentence serves more than one purpose.

2. Research Methodology/Research Design

Share with the reader of a very concise and summarized version of your Research Methodology/Research Design. If the important contribution of your work really is in the details of the methodology, you can and should provide those details in the Abstract and you can even give those details numerically. However, in many other cases the focus of the study is not on the methodology, in which case it is given in summary form and details are reserved for the Results. For example:

This study examines first–year undergraduate Australian and international engineering students as writers of academic texts in a multicultural setting at the University of Adelaide. A questionnaire and interviews were used to collect data about students' level of metalinguistic awareness, their attitudes toward, expectations for, assumptions about and motivation for writing.

3. Findings/Results

What are the key findings of your research? Ask yourself this question and list the answers one-by-one. After you have done this, write them out in the form of well-structured sentences that capture the main messages of your findings. For example:

The preliminary results of the research showed that students from different cultures initially have different concepts about the academic genres and handle writing with different learning and writing styles, but those with a more developed metalanguage are more confident and motivated. The conclusion can also be drawn that students' level of motivation for academic writing positively correlates with their opinion about themselves as writers.

One of the central functions of the Abstract is to emphasize new and important achievements of the study. Almost all Abstracts also include positive language at this point (an accurate determination) to demonstrate the value of the work.

4. Recommendations/Implication/Significance

This is where you give a summary of your Recommendations/Implication/ Significance. Let us say that you have a total of ten points offered in your dissertation. Do not list all ten of the Recommendations/Implication/Significance. Instead, summarize them into main ideas and write out short and concise sentences on these main ideas. For example:

Advocates for women's safety and rights should widen their net to include the new media and advocacy should be aimed at relevant ministries that work with both women's groups and centers of incarceration. Efforts at re-education and sensitization of inmates should be handled by authorities and other relevant ministries. Additionally, a public service should be offered to educate women on self-defense, legal rights and legal procedures.

Three sentences would be a good guideline to follow when writing your Recommendations/Implication/Significance in the Abstract, depending upon the word limit guidelines.

5. Conclusion

Keep your conclusion to one sentence. A good idea would be to mention future research as a conclusion in the context of a dissertation. For example:

Future research may include longitudinal studies of changing the perception of women among male perpetrators, immediate mental health needs of male perpetrators and gender differences.

Another option for a conclusion would be to share the limitations and how future research on the topic could avoid these limitations. For example:

Lack of good translation of the native language of participants hampered deeper probing of the issues surrounding incarceration of perpetrators. Future research would include questions written in the native language of respondents and the engagement of professional translation services.

The above two statements may be acceptable if you want to use them in a personal context. In the context of an academic paper that is submitted for publication, a conclusion may or may not be necessary depending on the publication. You examine past dissertations at your university for abstracts that are clear, concise and well written. Another good hint is to look at papers published in the academic journal you are aiming to publish in and examine what is the standard format used.

Vocabulary and Sentence Pattern for the Abstract

1. Background

a number of studies exist(s)	it is known that
frequently	it is widely accepted that
generally	occur(s)
is a common technique	often
is/are assumed to	popular
is/are based on	produce(s)
is/are determined by	recent research
is/are influenced by	recent studies
is/are related to	recently
it has recently been shown that	recently-developed

Aim

in order to	to examine
our approach	to investigate
the aim of this study	to study
to compare	with the aim of

Problem

(an) alternative approach	impractical
a need for	inaccurate
although	inconvenient
complicated	it should be possible to
desirable	limited
difficulty	not able to
disadvantage	problem
drawback	require
essential	risk
expensive	time-consuming
however	unsuccessful

2. Methodology/Materials

was/were assembled	was/were modelled
was/were calculated	was/were performed
was/were constructed	was/were recorded
was/were evaluated	was/were studied
was/were formulated	was/were treated
was/were measured	was/were used

3. Results

caused	was/were identified
decreased	was/were achieved
had no effect	was/were found
increased	was/were identical
it was noted/observed that...	was/were observed
occurred	was/were obtained
produced	was/were present
yielded	was/were unaffected (by)
resulted in	

Achievement/Contribution

accurate	achieve
consistent	allow
enhanced	demonstrate
improved	ensure
novel	guarantee
significant	obtain
suitable	validate
superior	compare well with
	in good agreement

Implications

The evidence/These results...	it is thought that
indicate(s) that	we conclude that
mean(s) that	we suggest that
suggest(s) that	may

4. Applications/Limitations and Future Work

applicability	make it possible to
can be applied	a preliminary attempt
can be used	not significant

	continue
slightly future directions potential use	relevant for/in future work

Creating a Title

Many more people will read the title than the Abstract, and many more will read the Abstract than the whole paper. This is because the title, like the Abstract, tells readers whether or not the research article will be useful for them. A good title will attract readers and, more importantly, will attract the appropriate readers. The reverse is also true: if the title is poor, the research article may not reach the appropriate audience. Start by looking at your research aim or the question you were trying to answer. Try and turn the question or problem into a title. For example,

What is the difference between x and y? ———▶ *A comparison of x and y*

How does x affect y? ———▶ *The effect of x on y*

The title should predict and describe the content of the paper as accurately as possible. The purpose of composing a good research title is to condense the paper's content in a few words, to capture the readers' attention and to differentiate the paper from other papers of the same subject area.

A typical title is usually composed of subject matter, key words of the method, and key words of the content.

Method	Content	Subject matter
Compare	Causes	Computer hackers
Analyze	Effects	Lung cancer
Contrast	Advantages	Nuclear power plant
Discuss	Benefits	Energy
Evaluate	Effectiveness	
Study		
Assess		

Good titles are usually concise, so it is not common to begin with phrases such as A study of... or An investigation into... They are also written in very formal English, so the use of a question mark is not common.

* An Analysis of Psychological Motivation of Computer Hackers

* The comparison of the Effectiveness of Two Approaches to Lung Cancer

* The Study of Environmental Effects of Nuclear Power Plants

Appropriate titles:

Psychological Motivation of Computer Hackers

Effectiveness of Two Approaches to Lung Cancer

Environmental Effects of Nuclear Power Plants

The following are the tips for writing the Title in the right form:

- Write the title in the middle of the first line.
- Capitalize the first word of the title and all the notional words in the title. The form words, such as articles, coordinating conjunctions, prepositions and the "to" in infinitives should not be capitalized, except the form words containing more than five words, like "without" "between" and "underneath" etc.
- No period is used at the end of a title.
- Use a question mark if the title is a direct question, but do not use one if it is an indirect question. e.g., Underline (or italicize if you use a computer) the names of books.
- Skip a line between the title and the first line of your paper.
- The first sentence should stand independent of the title. Do not use the words in the title to make up the opening sentence.

Exercises

I. Match the following statements with the names of the parts of the Abstract.

| Background | Method | Result | Significance | Conclusion |

1. To answer this question, we compared the performance of 12 novices (medical students) with the performance of 12 laparoscopic surgeons (using a 2D view) and 4 robotic surgeons, using a new robotic system that slows 2D and 3D view.

2. Our results showed a trivial effect of expertise. Results also revealed that experts have adaptive transfer capacities and are able to transfer their skills independently of the human-machine system. However, the expert's performance many be disturbed by changes in their usual environment.

3. Children undergoing long-term hospital care face problems of isolation from their familiar home and school environments. This isolation has an impact on the emotional well-being of the child.

4. Through this nuanced picture, the article urges those involved in teaching and researching second languages to recognize learners as more rounded individual persons.

5. The research provides new insights into how technology can support connectedness and provides a foundation for contributing to the wellbeing of children and young people in sensitive settings.

II. Rewrite the following titles in the right form.

1. Are children smarter because of the Internet?

2. The dangers of breast implants for teenagers.

3. Securing Internet commerce: is it possible in today's arms race of hackers and evolving technology?

III. Read the following Abstract part and match each sentence with a short description of what the writer is doing.

Physical properties of crude oil from acoustic measurements	
Abstract	In this sentence, the writer:
1. The speed of sound in a fluid is determined by, and therefore an indicator of, the thermodynamic properties of that fluid.	1_____
2. The aim of this study was to investigate the use of an ultrasonic cell to determine crude oil properties, in particular oil density.	2_____
3. An ultrasonic cell was constructed to measure the speed of sound and tested in a crude oil sample.	3_____
4. The speed of sound was measured at temperatures between 260 and 411K at pressures up to 75 MPs.	4_____
5. The measurements were shown to lead to an accurate determination of the bubble point of the oil.	5_____
6. This indicates that there is a possibility of obtaining fluid density from sound speed measurements and suggests that it is possible to measure sound absorption with an ultrasonic cell to determine oil viscosity.	6_____

IV. Write an Abstract.

Imagine that you and your team have designed a machine which can remove chewing gum from floors and pavements by treating the gum chemically to transform it into powder and then using vacuum suction to remove it.

In the Introduction, you began by saying that chewing gum removal is a significant environmental problem. You then provided factual information about the composition of chewing gum and the way in which it sticks to the floor. After that, you looked at existing chewing gum removal machines and noted that research has shown that they are unable to use suction to remove gum without damaging the floor surface. You referred to Gumbo et al., who claimed that it was possible to use chemicals to dissolve chewing gum. At the end of the Introduction you announced that you and your research team had designed a chewing gum removal machine (CGRM), which you call GumGone. GumGone sprays a non-toxic chemical onto the gum which transforms it to white powder. The machine can then remove the gum using suction without damaging the floor surface.

In the Methodology you described the design and construction of the machine. You compared your CGRM, GumGone, to two existing machines, Gumsucker and Vacu-Gum. You then gave details of a set of trials which you conducted to test the efficiency of the new CGRM and a further set of trials which showed the effect on the floor surface of gum removal.

In the Results section, you showed results of these trials. You compared the performance of GumGone with Gumsucker and Vacu-Gum. Your results were very good, and they can be seen in the tables below.

Table 1: Gum removal as a percentage of total sample

	Gumsucker	Vacu-gum	GumGone
Wooden floor	77	73	80
Stone floor	78	78	82
Carpeted floor	56	44	79

Table 2: Floor damage/staining

	Gumsucker	Vacu-gum	GumGone
Wooden floor	Minimal	Minimal	None
Stone floor	Significant	Some	None
Carpeted floor	Significant	Significant	Minimal

Discussion

Gum removal technology has traditionally faced the problem of achieving effective gum removal with minimal damage to floor surfaces. Existing CGRMs such as Gumsucker and Vacu-Gum use steam heat and steam injection respectively to remove gum and although both are fairly effective, the resulting staining and damage to floor surfaces, particularly carpeted floors, is often significant.

In this study the design and manufacture of a novel CGRM, GumGone, is presented. GumGone reduces the gum to a dry powder using a non-toxic chemical spray and then vacuums the residue, leaving virtually no stain. In trials, GumGone removed a high percentage of gum from all floor surfaces without causing floor damage. The floor surfaces tested included carpeted floors, suggesting that this technology is likely to have considerable commercial use.

Percentage removal levels achieved using GumGone were consistently higher than for existing CGRMs on all types of floor surface. This was particularly noticeable in the case of carpeted floor, where 79% of gum was removed from a 400m^2 area, as opposed to a maximum of 56% with existing machines. It represents a dramatic increase in the percentage amount of gum removed. Our results confirm the theory of Gumbo et al. that chemicals can be used to dissolve gum into dry powder and make it suitable for vacuuming.

The greatest advantage over existing CGRMs, however, lies in the combination of the two technologies in a single machine. By reducing the delay period between gum treatment and gum removal, the GumGone system resulted in negligible staining of floor surfaces. It represents a new approach which removes the need for stain treatment or surface repair following gum removal.

As noted earlier, only one wattage level (400 watts of vacuum suction power) was available in the GumGone prototype. Further work is needed to determine the power level at which gum removal is maximized and floor damage remains negligible.

参考答案

Chapter One   Principles of English Writing

Unit 1   Word Choice

Answers for Reference

IV. Rewrite the following passage and delete unnecessary words.

1. The tricolor pottery of the Tang dynasty is best known among people for its exquisite designs, brilliant colors, and vivid images. Making the pottery involves more than 30 processes, which is quite a large number. Baked twice at different temperatures, the clay bases are accented with soft glazes in the colors of amber, green and yellow. Tang pottery was used mainly as burial objects for the dead in ancient China, a custom that has kept many of these old and ancient relics from being destroyed across the centuries that have passed since they were first made so very long ago. Each year, archaeologists unearth from the ground more magnificent works from the period of the Tang dynasty. These priceless works are a part of China's priceless artistic heritage.

2. If you wish to experience a traditional time-honored Chinese celebration, there are few better choices you can make than the Dragon Boat Festival that falls on the fifth day of the fifth lunar month. This annual event started as part of a ceremonial ritual to commemorate the death of Qu Yuan, a minister of the government during the Warring States Period who is revered and esteemed for his integrity and patriotism. Dragon boat races are the most excitingly thrilling part of the festival, drawing huge crowds of spectators who watch them. Dragon boats are simply canoes that are decorated to look like open-mouthed dragons. The longest boats are powered by as many as 80 strong rowers. The winner is the first team to grab a flag at the finish point when the race comes to an end.

Unit 2　Sentence Effectiveness

Answers for Reference

III. Combine the following simple sentences into one complex sentence.

1. In a remote and dangerous motel, manager Norman Bates tries to protect his mother, who seems overly fond of knives.

2. A showman captures a giant ape in the jungle and takes him to New York City, where he escapes but dies fighting for the beautiful young woman he loves.

3. When Rick, a cynical American café owner in Casablanca, helps his former love and her husband, a French resistance fighter, he regains his self-respect.

Unit 3　Paragraph Development

Answers for Reference

Open

Chapter Two　Social Letters

Unit 4　Invitations

Answers for Reference

I. Read the following Invitation and match each part with a short description of what the writer is doing.

A. 1. Salutation　　2. Invitation　　3. Time
　　4. Place　　5. Additional information, Preferred dress

B. 1. Salutation　　2. Reason for the occasion
　　3. Time and Place　　4. Pleasure in seeing the person　　5. Closing signature

II. Write Invitations based on the information given in both formal and informal style.

Formal Invitation:

Dear Mr. Song,

To celebrate the 10th anniversary of TT Express, we are holding a dinner party at the Garden Hotel in Hangzhou on October 9. We sincerely invite you to attend the party.

You are the long-term partner and friend of our company. We hope to express our heartfelt appreciation to you for your generous support in so many years. We believe that our friendship and cooperation will last forever.

We are looking forward to seeing you at the party.

Faithfully yours,
Li Guang, Marketing Manager
TT Express

Informal Invitation: Open

Unit 5 Thank-you Letters

Answers for Reference

I. Read the following Thank-you letters and match each part with a short description of what the writer is doing.

A. 1. First Thank you   2. Reasons   3. Offer to return the favor

B. 1. First Thank you   2. Reasons

3. Close with gratitude again, with a few words unrelated to the object

II. Write Thank-you letters based on the information given.

1.

Dear Mr. Black,

Thanks for your help in supporting our seminar and making it a great success.

Your company has been in a long-term cooperation with ours in nearly 5 years. You lent us technological support and suggestions on almost all our seminars and exhibitions. We sincerely appreciate that.

Thank you again and look forward to the next cooperation.

Faithfully yours,
Yang Shujie
Manager of Public Relations
C&C Information Technology Co., Ltd

2.

Dear Mrs. Wang,

Thank you so much for the gift book you gave to my son. He loves the book so much that he reads and shares the stories with us every day. It is exactly what he needs.

Thanks for your kindness again.

Sincerely yours,
Janet

3.

Dear Vincent Crumm,

Thank you for your contribution of $200 to the Alumni Annual Giving Campaign.

As stipulated on the donor card returned to this office, your gift will be designated for the Annual Giving Fund to be used where most needed.

We also appreciate your use of the Langdon Co. matching gifts program and look forward to receiving their one-for-one matching gift. This matching gift will also be directed to the Annual Giving Fund.

Thank you again for your generosity, which will make it possible for many young women and young men to have the advantage of a quality education.

Very truly yours,
Alex Diazon

Unit 6 Apologies

Answers for Reference

I. Read the following Apologies and match each part with a short description of what the writer is doing.

A. 1. First Apology 2. Reasons and explanations   3. Corrective action and second Apology

B. 1. Thanks for bring the problem to attention 2. Explanation and first Apology
  3. Corrective action   4. Second Apology

II. Write Apologies based on the information given.

1.

Dear Annette,

I must beg your forgiveness for my outspoken and insensitive remarks last night about your religious convictions. I'm afraid I got carried away in the heat of the discussion. I certainly feel that each of us has a right to our own beliefs, and I in no way meant to belittle yours.

I would be happy if you would accept an invitation to dinner at my house on Saturday, August 3, at 7:00 p.m. I'm just having a few friends, most of whom you know.

Hoping to see you then.

Yours truly,
(writer's name)

2.

Dear Steven,

My comments about your playing last Thursday had only the best intention. Any suggestions I make are only to make you a better player. You're already so good, I didn't think my suggestion would upset you.

I am sorry my words upset you. From now on, I'll think more carefully about how I say things before I say them. My job is to teach and motivate you, and I let you down in the latter. My apologies.

Sincerely,

(writer's name)

3.

Dear Sir or Madam,

We are unable to deliver the spring fabric samples by the date promised. The product supervisor promises me that you will have them by January 5. If this is unsatisfactory, please telephone me. It isn't often we have to renege on a delivery date, and we're not happy about it. Please accept our apologies for the delay.

Sincerely,

(writer's name)

Unit 7 Congratulations

Answers for Reference

I. Read the following Congratulations and match each part with a short description of what the writer is doing.

A. 1. Congratulations   2. Reflection on the issue   3. Wish of success

B. 1. Congratulations   2. Wish of success   3. Continued business cooperation and support

II. Write Congratulations based on the information given.

1.

Dear Annie,

Congratulations on receiving the Elite Student award! That's terrific. I was so happy for you when I saw the announcement in the paper.

I hope everything else in your life is going well too.

Best,

(writer's name)

2.

Dear Helen and Arthur,

So little Laura has arrived at last. It has been such a long process, and I know it's been hard for you. But all that's over now, and the three of you can begin your life together.

From what I hear, this is definitely an adoption made in heaven. I know that Laura will add a great deal to the joy you two already find in each other. Congratulations!

With every good wish.

Yours,
(writer's name)

3.

Dear Mr. Rochester,

Congratulations on your election to the Greenfield School Board. All of us who campaigned for you in this area are proud and pleased to have been part of your victory.

Please accept my best wishes for a distinguished, productive, and happy term of office.

Respectfully yours,
(writer's name)

Unit 8　Application

Answers for Reference

I. Read the following Application letters and match each part with a short description of what the writer is doing.

A. 1. Purpose of the letter 2. List the skills 3. Request for an interview and offer contact

B. 1. Qualification for the position 2. List the skills 3. Willingness to an interview

II. Write Application letters based on the positions offered, and add source of information, related skills, reasons of application, contact information etc., which are necessary for an Application.

1.

Dear Ms. Silver,

As the result of a telephone call to your office this morning, I learned that Duval International is seeking someone to manage the security operations of its office complex, and that you are the person to contact about the position.

I have eleven years' experience as a security services supervisor and broad experience with access control and with most security systems, including CCTV alarms. I also have an AA degree in law enforcement.

I was employed by S&T from 1989~1994, and by Box associates from 1994 to the present. Favorable references are available from both companies.

I would like to set up an interview to discuss the position with you. I have 24-hour voice mail at 555-1234.

2.

Dear Mr. Hanm,

I saw in yesterday's New York Times that you are looking for a receptionist for your new office at Center Plaza. My background is wonderfully matched with your requirement.

You ask for fluency in seven languages because people of all nations may work with your company. I am of Danish birth, brought up by a Danish father and Greek mother in Paris, and schooled in French. Then, I moved with my family to Italy and later to Russia, where my father was employed in the foreign service of Denmark.

I was fortunate to be able to continue my studies in the United States and have therefore an excellent knowledge of English. I studied both Italian and Spanish and acquired fluency both written and spoken. Thus, I have a good command of seven languages.

I enjoy working with different cultures. I am experienced with budgets, schedules, and general coordination of routines, and I consider myself to have a good judgment of people and situations. I feel confident that the position which you describe, is one for which I am suited, and which would give me great pleasure.

I am enclosing some references for you. I shall try to contact you next week and I would like to talk with you about the feasibility of working at Center Plaza.

Yours sincerely,
(writer's name)

3.

Dear Mr. Bally,

The requirements for the branch manager position you advertised describe almost perfectly my own background. As the assistant manager of XX Travel, I have been responsible for overseeing eight full-time agents. I am a travel school graduate with a great deal of experience and a good working knowledge of the travel industry in all its phases—from issuing tickets and seat assignments and assisting with ticket assembly to computer experience. I have two years of experience in domestic reservations, one year of experience working with corporate international travel operations, and a thorough understanding of international tariffs.

I would like to discuss this position with you and will be happy to come in for an interview at your convenience.

Sincerely yours,
(writer's name)

Unit 9　Résumé

I. Open

II. Open

Unit 10　Recommendation

I. Read the following Recommendation letters and match each part with a short description of what the writer is doing.

　A. 1. State the connection　　2. State the qualified working ability

　　　3. Be willing to provide further information

　B. 1. Recommendation and Statement of connection

　　　2. Detailed examples of positive work habits

　　　3. Reaffirm the recommendation

II. Write Recommendation letters based on the information given.

1.

Department of the SPECIAL CLASS GIFTED for YOUTHS

University of Science and Technology

Hefei, Anhui 230026, P.R. China

July 1, 2018

Dear Sir or Madam,

　　I take great pleasure in recommending Wang Yong, one of my favorite students, for admission into your distinguished graduate program.

　　Mr. Wang was admitted in 2006 at the age of 14 into the SPECIAL CLASS for the GIFTED YOUTHS, my university's unique program that caters to the intellectual needs of unusually talented Chinese youngsters. It was a rare privilege he earned with his nearly impeccable academic performance through the years of his elementary and secondary school.

　　He impressed me almost as he entered into my university, a major cradle of China's scientific and technological talents. At the time, members of the Gifted Class all had to spend half a month studying by themselves the principles of calculus and then take an exam so that we could evaluate their self-study capability. Mr. Wang scored the highest grade in that exam. He also exhibited a keenly active mind during class discussions. To my regret at the time, his English was not as good as his mathematics or physics. But I noticed he made a point of working especially hard in improving his English during his five undergraduate years with us. By now, he seems to be at least as proficient in English as most of his former classmates in the Gifted Class.

　　In my experience with Mr. Wang, I was impressed with not only his extraordinary intelligence but also his ambitions and persistence. I am sure that Mr. Wang will be an outstanding student in any doctoral program that he may care to enroll in. So I would like to support him firmly and would greatly appreciate it you decide to accept him as he wishes.

Yours sincerely,

(writer's name)

College of Computer Science, ABC University

2.

To whom it may concern,

It gives me a great pleasure to recommend Mr. Deng as a transfer to the School of Business Administration of your University in the summer quarter of 2019. During the academic years of 2010~2014, he was a student in our Department, World College of Journalism. I found him very diligent and intelligent. He often participated in extracurricular activities, contributing a great deal to community affairs. Though Mr. Deng graduated from this college 5 years ago, he keeps contact with me very often. Worthy of mention also is his personality, honest, reliable, responsible and mature. I strongly recommend this promising young man and your favorable consideration and assistance to him will be very much appreciated.

your faithfully,

(writer's name)

Department of Management, ABC University

Chapter Three   Business Correspondence

Unit 11   Requests and Inquiries

Answers for Reference

Open

Unit 12   Orders

Answers for Reference

I. Choose the appropriate word or words.

1. shipment, ordered   2. firm, within   3. in   4. on   5. terms, place, to   6. send, specifications   7. in, cancel   8. accept, arrangements   9. acknowledge

II. Fill in the blanks with the phrases in is the box.

1. In accordance with   2. place regular orders   3. in duplicate   4. in case

5. in one's favor   6. shipment   7. together with

III. Translate the following sentences into English

1. We are very interested in the different models of bicycles you offer and have decided to place a trial order.

2. All the items are urgently required by our customers. We, therefore, hope you will make delivery at an early date.

3. The relevant L/C has been issued by Bank of China, Shanghai Branch. Upon receipt of the side, please arrange the shipment and inform us by fax of the name of vessel and the date of sailing.

4. Shipment will be made within 3 weeks from acceptance of your order. Our terms by payment are draft at sight under an irrevocable L/C. Marine insurance will be covered by us.

5. We acknowledge with thanks the receipt of Order No. WG721/BP dated 20th September.

6. We regret to say that we are unable to accept your order of 1,000 computers owing to heavy commitments.

IV. Read the below order letter carefully and then write a confirmation letter to the buyer.

Dear Sirs,

We have accepted your Order No. 16 for handkerchiefs, leather shoes and socks and we are sending you herewith our Sales Confirmation No. Garm-263 in duplicate. Would you please sign and return one copy to us for file?

It is understood that a letter of credit in our favor covering the above-mentioned goods will be established at once. Please note that the stipulations in the relevant credit should strictly conform to the terms stated in our Sales Confirmation so as to avoid subsequent amendments.

You may rest assured that we shall effect shipment with the least possible delay upon receipt of the credit.

We appreciate your cooperation and look forward to receiving your further orders.

Faithfully yours,

(writer's name)

Unit 13 Complaints

Answers for Reference

I. Translate the following sentences into English.

1. I know you will want to see that such an incident does not occur again.

2. It is my understanding that it will be repaired/replaced at your expense.

3. I would like a refund in the amount of $49.99.

4. I would like to clear up this misunderstanding as soon as possible.

5. We would like to resolve this difficulty without delay.

II. Write a letter of Complaints based on the following condition.

Dear Sirs,

Our order no. J733

We have received the documents and taken delivery of the goods which arrived at Port Elizabeth on the S.S. Castle yesterday.

We are much obliged to you for the prompt execution of this order. Everything seems to be correct and in good condition except in case 14. Unfortunately, when we opened this case we found it contained completely different articles from those ordered, and we can only presume that a mistake has been made and that this case is part of another order.

As we need the articles, we ordered to complete deliveries to our customers, we must ask you to arrange for replacements to be dispatched at once. We attach a list of the contents of case 14 and would be glad if you would check this against our order and your copy of the invoice. In the meantime, we are holding the case at your disposal; please let us know what you wish to do with it.

Yours faithfully,
(writer's name)

III. Write a Response letter to a customer's complaints based on the following condition.

Dear Ms. Poivre,

Thank you for your telephone call regarding your recent purchase of Mocha Cocoa Chip Ice Cream. We are sorry to hear that the ice cream lacked the quality you have come to expect from us. During our manufacturing process, added ingredients are mixed into the ice cream using a special feeder. In the case of your carton, it appears that we were the victims of human or mechanical error, in that the feeder failed to add the appropriate quantity of chocolate pieces to the mix. Please be assured that we have reported this incident to our quality assurance department and that they are implementing measures to ensure that this situation does not recur.

We are sorry that you were unable to enjoy your ice cream as a result. Please accept the enclosed gift certificate for one quart of our premium ice cream to replace your purchase. We hope that you will give us another chance to provide you with the quality ice cream you deserve and that all your future encounters with our ice cream bring you nothing but pleasure.

Warm regards,
(writer's name)

Enclosure: Certificate—One Quart

Unit 14 Appreciation

Answers for Reference

I. Translate the following sentences into English.

1. As principal of Jerome Elementary School, you might like to know that we think Miss Louisa is an absolute treasure.

2. I'd like to express my appreciation for the knowledgeable and sympathetic care you gave me during my hospitalization for bypass surgery.

3. I want to express my appreciation to all of you for the extra hours and hard work you put in last week to secure the HX contract.

4. I want to tell you how much I appreciate what you are doing for the garbage recycling program in our neighborhood.

5. This past year has been a banner year for the company, and you have contributed significantly to its success.

II. Write Letters of Appreciation on the conditions given.

1.

Dear Ms. Stanley,

The entire department joins me in expressing our appreciation to you for the superb workshop on hard disk filing system. We all learned a great deal. And I was especially fascinated by your introductory description of early SSS files. I am passing on your brochure to George Hickson in Building 201-B in case he would be interested in having you speak to his department.

Yours truly,
(writer's name)

2.

Dear Mr. Fitz,

We were pleased to learn that you received such outstanding service from one of our employees.

Be assured that we have passed on your compliments to Ms. Stretton. You will perhaps enjoy knowing that in recognition of her talent and managerial skills, Ms. Stretton has just been promoted to floor supervisor.

We appreciate your taking the time to write us.

Yours truly,
(writer's name)

Unit 15 Refusal

Answers for Reference

I. Translate the following sentences into English.

1. Although we appreciate your interest in M&M Toys, we do not feel that your product is the one we could successfully market.

2. I appreciate your offer, but I want to try a few things before I go outside the firm for a solution.

3. If you re-read your contract, specifically clause Cl, you will see that we have no legal obligations in this regard.

4. I hope this will help you understand why we are unable to furnish the additional funding you are requesting.

5. We have reviewed your credit application and regret to inform you that we are unable to offer you a bank card at this time.

II. Write letters of Refusal on the conditions given.

1.

Dear Daisy,

Thank you for your kind letter asking me to direct the annual fundraise. I am flattered that you thought of me.

Because of several other time-consuming commitments, I am unable to accept your invitation. I would have enjoyed working with you and contributing in some way to our fine library system, but I feel sure that you will find the right person for this important project.

With best wishes.

Sincerely yours,

(writer's name)

2.

Dear Tony Chrispy,

Thank you for submitting your work to us. As editors of BCD Review, we have given your material careful consideration; every manuscript submitted to this office is read by one or more of us.

We regret that "The Ninth Son" is not suited to the current needs of the magazine, but we wish to thank you for having given us the opportunity of reading it. Unfortunately, the volume of submissions and the press of other editorial responsibilities do not permit us to make individual comments or suggestions.

Sincerely,

(writer's name)

Chapter Four Research Paper

Unit 16 Introduce the Study

Answers for Reference

II. Read the text and finish the following writing tasks.

Task One

1. The development of transportation.

2. No studies addressing public perception and acceptance of this emerging technology, especially across several countries and its change over time, remain scarce.

3. RQ1: How can we measure public perceptions of self-driving cars to anticipate acceptance?

RQ2: How do events influence the public perception of self-driving cars?

4. We created an approach for automatically determining and monitoring perceived risks and benefits of emerging technologies from short 140-character text messages published on the social media platform Twitter.

5. First, we provide an overview of current literature on technology acceptance, self-driving cars, and previous research on the acceptance of self-driving cars. Second, we describe the data extraction from Twitter, the preprocessing of the data, and the model generation including its evaluation. Third, we describe and discuss the results of extracting the relevant data and applying our machine learning model to this data. We conclude with a summary of the results, limitations of our work, possibilities for further research, and the contributions to research and practice.

Task Two

1. background   2. previous studies   3. methodology   4. purpose   5. outline

III. Write an Introduction.

Task One

1. The writer establishes the importance of this research topic.

2. The writer provides general background information for the reader.

3. The writer does the same as in Sentences 1 and 2, but in a more specific /detailed way.

4. The writer describes the general problem area or the current research focus of the eld.

5. The writer provides a transition between the general problem area and the literature review.

6. The writer provides a brief overview of key research projects in this area.

7. The writer describes a gap in the research.

8. The writer describes the paper itself.

9. The writer gives details about the methodology reported in the paper.

10. The writer announces the findings.

Task Two

Sample Answer

A COVER FOR THE SPPPV (Single-Person Pedal-Powered Vehicle)

Concerns about global warming and urban air pollution have become central issues in transport policy decision-making, and as a result much research in recent years has focused on the development of vehicles which are environmentally friendly. Air quality in cities is currently significantly lower than in rural areas and this has been shown to be directly linked to the level of vehicle emissions from private cars. Due to the fact that urban transport policy in the UK is designed to reduce or discourage the use of private cars, there has been an increase in the sale of non-polluting vehicles such as the SPPPV (Single-Person Pedal-Powered Vehicle). However, although the number of SPPPV users has increased, safety and comfort issues need to be addressed if the number of users is to increase to a level at which a significant effect on environmental pollution can be achieved.

Researchers have studied and improved many aspects of the SPPPV. In 1980, Wang et al. responded to the need for increased safety by designing an SPPPV surrounded by a "cage" of safety bars, and in 2001 Martinez developed this further with the introduction of a reinforced polymer screen which could be fitted to the safety bars to protect the cyclist's face in the event of a collision. The issue of comfort has also been addressed by many design teams; in 1998 Kohl et al. introduced an SPPPV with a built-in umbrella, which could be opened at the touch of a button, and more recently, Martinez has added a mesh filter which can be placed over the entire cage to reduce the risk of environmental pollution. However, the resulting "cage" or cover is aerodynamically ineffective due to the shape of the umbrella and the weight of the mesh filter.

In this study, we used computer simulation to model the aerodynamic effect of the existing safety and comfort features and we present a new design which integrates these features in an optimally effective aerodynamic shape.

Unit 17 Develop Literature Review

Answers for Reference

III. Reading practice

Task One

1. The research is focused on the relationship between our eating behavior and

emotional states.

2. Introduction, body, conclusion and references.

3. In topical order.

4. Influence of mood on eating behavior, gender differences, influence of eating behavior on later moods, a Chronic Stress Response Network.

5. Dallman's study in 2005 and Tomiyama's study in 2011.

6. The comfort foods many of us indulge in when we are experiencing stress or sadness are aptly named.

Task Two

1. There has been much research on how the food we eat affects our physical health...(para.1)

2. Studies have found that... Research has also highlighted... Research has shown that(para.1)

3. In contrast, men who are not dieting likely...(para.6)

4. There are some areas of this research in need of more explanation.(para.3)
   There are some limits, however, to the findings of these studies.(para.10)

5. The next step should be to research...(para.12)

Unit 18 State the Methodology

Answers for Reference

I. Reading

Task One

1. Sentence 1 offers a general overview of the entire subsection, including the purpose of the investigation.

2. In sentence 2, the writer provides background information and justifies the choice of location by referring to previous research.

3. Sentence 3 provides an overview of the procedure/method itself.

4. Sentence 4 provides details about what was done and used and also shows that care was taken.

5. Sentence 5 continues to describe what was done in detail, using language which communicates that care was taken.

6. Sentence 6 describes what was done by referring to existing methods in the literature.

7. Sentence 7 provides more detail information about the method and shows it to have been a good choice.

8. Sentence 8 provides more details of the method.

9. Sentence 9 mentions a possible difficulty in the methodology.

II. Writing: Write a Methodology section.

Two experiments were carried out using different combinations of seasoning and varying cooking temperatures. A 4.5 kg frozen organic chicken was purchased from Buyrite Supermarket. Buyrite only sells grade "A" chickens approved by the Organic Farmers Association, thus ensuring both the homogeneity of the sample and the quality of the product. Seasonings were obtained from Season Inc UK and were used as supplied.

According to the method described by Hanks et al. (1998), the chicken was first immersed in freshly boiled water cooled to a temperature of 20°C and was subsequently rinsed thoroughly in a salt solution so as to reduce the level of bacteria on the surface of the chicken. In order to obtain two samples of equal size and weight for testing, the chicken was first skinned using a standard BS1709 Skin-o-matic; the flesh was then removed from the bone with a 4 cm steel Sabatier knife, which it was cut into 3 cm-cubes, each weighing 100g.

Two of the cubes thus obtained were randomly selected for testing. The cubes were dried individually in a Phillips R2D2 Dehydrator for 10 minutes. Immediately after removing each cube from the dehydrator it was coated with the selected seasoning mixture and left to stand on a glass plate for 30 minutes at room temperature (16 °C) in order to enhance absorption of the seasoning prior to heating. Seasoning quantities were measured by using standard domestic kitchen scales and were therefore only approximate.

Each cube was then placed on an ovenproof dish and transferred to a preheated Panasonic Model 33KY standard electric fan-assisted oven at 150 °C for 10 minutes. The product was removed from the oven and allowed to come to equilibrium, after which the cubes were assessed according to the TTS test developed by Dundee (Dundee, 1997).

Unit 19 Present Results and Findings

Answers for Reference

I. Reading.

Task One

1. 1) During the first 20 years, from 1935 to 1955, the pace of IMRAD increments was slow, from none to 20%. However, during the following 20 years, 1955 to 1975, the frequency of these articles more than quadrupled (Figure 1).

2) Figure 2 shows the text organization in the British Medical Journal from 1935 to 1985.

2. One interesting finding is that during the initial period of our study, the order of the IMRAD headings did not follow today's convention.

3. Information, which today is highly standardized in one section, would be absent, repeated, or dispersed among sections in earlier articles.

4. Location statement, important findings and brief comments.

Task Two

The authors did not find definite reasons explaining the leadership of the IMRAD structure in the literature. **It is possible** that sciences other than medicine **might** have influenced the growing use of this structure. The field of physics, for example, had already adopted it extensively in the 1950s.

This structure was already considered the ideal outline for scientific writing in the first quarter of the 20th century; however, it was not used by authors. After World War II, international conferences on scientific publishing recommended this format, culminating with the guidelines set by the International Committee of Medical Journal Editors, formerly **known as** the Vancouver Group, first published in the late 1970s. According to Huth, the wide use of the IMRAD structure **may be** largely credited to editors, who insisted on papers being clearly formatted to benefit readers and to facilitate the process of peer review.

Four major leading journals of internal medicine were examined. It **might be assumed** that patterns set by these journals would be followed by others; nevertheless, caution **should** be taken in extrapolating these findings to other journals.

II. Writing.

Sample Answer

Results

Based on the assumption that the timing of UFO sightings may be of significance, the aim of this study was to investigate a possible link between the number of UFO sightings close to the epicenter during the period immediately prior to an earthquake, and the earthquakes that follow.

The process of evaluating UFO sightings is complex and time-consuming. Checks with police, air traffic control operators and meteorologists were performed. Where possible, witnesses were interviewed and videos of the area was examined in order to eliminate as many conventional explanations as possible, such as satellites, meteors, space debris and even bird flocks. All the cases were documented using the procedure followed by Vader and results are displayed in Table 1. The Richter scale was used to measure magnitude.

It is evident from the results that overall, there was a marked increase in sightings during the seven days prior to the earthquake. These results are in line with those of Kenobi et al. (2004), who noted a mean fourfold increase worldwide. In Russia and the USA, for example, the number of sightings increased approximately fourfold during the week preceding the earthquake, and in Canada the increase was even more dramatic. Although the number of sightings is low in Canada, this may have been due to a low national interest in UFOs; in addition, the earthquake took place in a sparsely-populated area of the country. It is significant that almost all the participants in each country gave exactly the same description of "their" UFO, and that these descriptions were noticeably different from those obtained in other countries.

It appears from this evidence that the period immediately prior to earthquake activity was associated with an increase in the number of UFO sightings. However, this work represents only a preliminary attempt to establish such a link. The actual relationship between the two may be more complex; for example, it is possible that because a Star Wars film was released in the USA during the period under study, the number of sightings was higher that week without any real change in UFO activity. These results nevertheless suggest that monitoring UFO activity may provide useful input for earthquake prediction strategies.

Unit 20 Compose Discussion/Conclusion

Answers for Reference

I. Rewrite these sentences by using tentative language.

1. It is assumed that playing violent video games may cause more aggression, bullying, and fighting.

2. Mars is certainly the focus of much scientific study and often considered the foremost planet for human colonization.

3. It could be the case that certain news reports can never be trusted because of the possibility of media bias, journalist interpretation and agenda setting.

4. It is generally believed that climate change is caused by human activities.

II. Read the Discussion and Conclusion part of a thesis and finish the following writing tasks.

Task One

1. Paragraph 1.

2. Paragraph 2~6.

3. The study reported here was carried out on a relatively small scale and it would not be fair to make any broad generalizations based on what we found.

4. Our research suggests four specific teacher cognitions that might be more widely disseminated:

(1) Most (and probably all) teachers face ISKD situations.

(2) The occurrence of an ISKD situation does not necessarily reflect poorly on the

teacher.

(3) There are many ways of dealing with ISKD.

(4) ESP teachers, subject specialist teachers and students are all potential sources of information about the subject specialism and its language.

Task Two

7. The study reported here was carried out on a **relatively** small scale and it **would not be** fair to make any broad generalizations based on what we found. **We would like to suggest**, however, that it **may** have implications for teacher development within the context in which the research was carried out and, **possibly**, more widely. Despite the influence of the local educational culture, teacher cognitions and practices do vary. The two risk taking episodes indicate that there is, **at least**, **the possibility** for teachers to develop new ways of dealing with ISKDS that are culturally appropriate and pedagogically sound. Our research suggests four specific teacher cognitions that **might** be more widely disseminated.

III. Write a Discussion/Conclusion.

Sample Answer

Discussion

Gum removal technology has traditionally faced the problem of achieving effective gum removal with minimal damage to floor surfaces. Existing CGRMs such as Gumsucker and Vacu-Gum use steam heat and steam injection respectively to remove gum and although both are fairly effective, the resulting staining and damage to floor surfaces, particularly carpeted floors, is often significant.

In this study the design and manufacture of a novel CGRM, GumGone, is presented. GumGone reduces the gum to a dry powder using a non-toxic chemical spray and then vacuums the residue, leaving virtually no stain. In trials, GumGone removed a high percentage of gum from all floor surfaces without causing floor damage. The floor surfaces tested included carpeted floors, suggesting that this technology is likely to have considerable commercial use.

Percentage removal levels achieved using GumGone were consistently higher than for existing CGRMs on all types of floor surface. This was particularly noticeable in the case of carpeted floor, where 79% of gum was removed from a 400 m^2 area, as opposed to a maximum of 56% with existing machines. It represents a dramatic increase in the percentage amount of gum removed. Our results confirm the theory of Gumbo et al. that chemicals can be used to dissolve gum into dry powder and make it suitable for vacuuming.

The greatest advantage over existing CGRMs, however, lies in the combination of the two technologies in a single machine. By reducing the delay period between gum treatment and gum removal, the GumGone system resulted in negligible staining of floor surfaces. It represents a new approach which removes the need for stain treatment or surface repair following gum removal.

As noted earlier, only one wattage level (400 watts of vacuum suction power) was available in the GumGone prototype. Further work is needed to determine the power level at which gum removal is maximized and floor damage remains negligible.

Unit 21　Write the Abstract

Answers for Reference

I. Match the following statements with the names of the parts of the Abstract.

1. Method　2. Result　3. Introduction　4. Conclusion　5. Significance

II. Rewrite the following titles in the right form.

1. Are Children Smarter Because of the Internet?

2. The Dangers of Breast Implants for Teenagers.

3. Securing Internet Commerce: Is it Possible in Today's Arms Race of Hackers and Evolving Technology?

III. Read the following Abstract part and match each sentence with a short description of what the writer is doing.

1. The writer provides background factual information.

2. The writer combines the method, the general aim and the specific aim of the study in one sentence.

3. The writer summarizes the methodology and provides details.

4. The writer indicates the achievement of the study.

5. The writer presents the implications of the study.

IV. Write an Abstract.

Sample Answer

Abstract

The fats and resins in chewing gum contribute to elasticity, bulk and texture but also increase staining. The aim of this study was to design a gum removal machine able to remove gum chemically with no stain residue. A machine, GumGone, was designed and constructed, which injected non-ionic detergent into gum deposits using a power spray and then immediately vacuumed the resulting powder. It was found that 1 μl of detergent achieved effective, stain-free removal over a 300m^2 area. Performance was superior to existing systems and suggests that the delay between treatment and removal is a significant factor in staining.